Shakespeare – The Barriers Removed

Studymates

British History 1870–1918
Warfare 1792–1918
Hitler and Nazi Germany (3rd Edition)
English Reformation
European History 1870–1918
Genetics (2nd edition)
Lenin, Stalin and Communist Russia
Organic Chemistry
Chemistry: As Chemistry Explained
Chemistry: Chemistry Calculations Explained
The New Science Teacher's Handbook
Mathematics for Adults
Calculus
Understanding Forces
Algebra: Basic Algebra Explained
Plant Physiology
Poems to Live By
Shakespeare
Poetry
Better English
Better French
Better German
Better Spanish
Social Anthropology
Statistics for Social Science
Practical Drama and Theatre Arts
The War Poets 1914–18
The Academic Essay
Your Master's Thesis
Your PhD Thesis

Shakespeare – The Barriers Removed

Paul Innes

© 2005 by Paul Innes

ISBN 10 1-84 285-051-0
ISBN 13 978 1-84 285-051-0

First published in 2005 by Studymates Limited.
PO Box 225, Abergele, LL18 9AY, United Kingdom.

Website: http://www.studymates.co.uk

Typeset by Domex e-Data Pvt. Ltd.
Printed and bound in Great Britain by Baskerville Press

For Cathy: the first of many

Contents

Preface

This book is intended to bring the general reader up to date with recent developments in Shakespeare studies. It has been structured so as to introduce students beginning a higher-education course on Shakespeare to the kinds of things they will be expected to know. However, the chapters are organised as a logical progression from familiar terms to more advanced issues. Readers who are not taking a course on Shakespeare will still find themselves moving into areas of discussion they perhaps had not been involved with before.

Formal study of Shakespeare at this level requires focus. It is not enough simply to be interested in Shakespeare's works; it is at least as important to organise your time and energy in a way that has beneficial effects upon your coursework. And if you find yourself becoming more interested in other aspects of literary and dramatic studies, at least you will be able to survive your encounter with this particular playwright.

Pragmatic considerations are therefore paramount. This book has chapters on characterisation, setting, performance and so on, but it also suggests ways of dealing with secondary material. This is the big difference between any prior experience you may already have had, and what you will be expected to do now. You will not simply be studying the plays or poems; you will be asked to engage with the broader issues raised by them. Ultimately, precisely how you deal with your Shakespeare requirements is up to you. Also, therefore, are the ways in which you utilise the ideas contained within this book. Always remember to keep a sense of proportion in relation to your other courses.

Each chapter ends with a Tutorial section. These tutorials suggest ideas on how to study effectively and also provide you with a selection of standard assessment questions. The tenth chapter is itself a large tutorial. This combination should give you a good idea of a standard course format. Remember, *how* you study is at least as important as *what* you study. Towards the end of the book you will find six chapters on the most commonly studied plays. These chapters provide extremely detailed practical breakdowns of each play. These breakdowns relate the action to the kinds of issues that come up in discussion, lectures and assessments. They also present the plays in discrete, easily digestible pieces, enabling you to see at a glance how they are constructed.

Finally, this book raises issues that you will be expected to develop for yourself in a more advanced or specialised course on Shakespeare. *Studymates* has its own website, where you can contact the author of this book for further information.

Paul Innes

E-mail: *paulinnes@studymates.co.uk*

Note: The edition of Shakespeare's works that is used throughout this book is *The Reverside Shakespeare* (Houghton Mifflin Company, 1997, 2nd edition).

Getting Started

What You Already Know (and What You Don't)

Many people will have already encountered the works of Shakespeare one way or another – usually at school. School leavers have traditionally constituted the vast majority of university students. But they are now being joined by different kinds of students, who come from overseas or start their studies later. There has always been this sort of mixture in most universities, but the mix is becoming more apparent. Some mature students may be retired, and coming back to education out of interest. Others may be in their twenties or thirties, returning to education after time with families or at work. Still others may be taking their courses on day release from full or part–time employment. Then there are those who are not involved in formal education, but wish to pursue a topic that interests them.

Students who have just finished their A-Levels or equivalent will not necessarily have an advantage over the others. This is especially true when dealing with a dramatist such as Shakespeare. Think of school study as a training regime. Students are not usually encouraged to think independently. They are trained to pass through a certain kind of examination system. Therefore, any formal education you may have had will only be a basic level of preparation for what now faces you. Students who are not starting from this position will probably have a wider life experience. Many will have had more chance to absorb elements of Shakespeare, possibly by going to the theatre by themselves. They will not necessarily have been shepherded there as part of a school course.

All of this may seem straightforward. But universities do not make life easy for you. You will probably be part of a huge year intake and most of your study will take the form of mass lectures. This system will be supplemented by the occasional small-group tutorial. You will be expected to go to libraries yourself, although you will probably be given adequate reading lists. You will have to write a large number of essays across all of your courses, pretty much at the same time. You will also have a run of exams in different subjects close to one another. And in the midst of all this, you will be the one expected to organise your study time.

This book is intended to help you navigate through a difficult subject in a way that puts you in control of your time and material. This is the secret to university study, and it is surprisingly obvious. How you deal with your time is at least as important as the books you study. With Shakespeare, you will be pushed to advance your ideas beyond your previous experience. The single most difficult thing about starting a higher-education course is the difference between what you already know and what you will be required to develop for yourself.

Your Course of Study

There are three basic course structures for studying English literature at this level. The first is the survey course, which can last a whole year. These typically begin around the Renaissance, or even earlier. They give you a snapshot of important periods in literary history as a basis for later years of study. Such courses usually include one or two Shakespeare plays. Although Shakespeare is not a major component of the course, the chances are that you will have to write your first essay on one of his plays.

The second type of course structure is the period course, and this is often quite an intensive study of one group of writers. If your course is one of these, and if it includes Shakespeare, then you will definitely need this book. You will probably be at a university that begins its introduction to literary studies with the English Renaissance. Shakespeare's period will serve as the chronological basis for later study. You will have to deal not only with several of Shakespeare's works, but also with those of his contemporaries. Many of the comments you will find in Chapter 7 should help with a course such as this.

The third course structure you could be faced with is one based on genre. Typically, these divide the academic year into groups of topics such as poetry, the novel and drama. Shakespeare could come into at least one of these. The rationale behind this kind of course structure is an open one. It does not assume that all students have the same prior experience of study. Once a thorough basis of genre study is established, future years will extend the material for study. As with the first model discussed above, Shakespeare will be only a minor part of this type of structure, at least to begin with.

How to Cope

Rationalise. Decide for yourself how important each course segment really is. Are you going to spend a lot of time on Shakespeare? Or are you going to wing it, so that you can concentrate on something elsewhere in your curriculum that is weaker? This book will give you pointers on how to integrate Shakespeare studies with your own particular environment. And finally, don't panic. One poor grade is not the end of the world. Most course systems have an in-built safety net, whether it be continuous assessment or examination resits. If you decide to continue with Shakespeare in later years, you will probably move beyond the scope of this book. You will have developed your own ideas, which is the whole point of education.

This Book

As you move through this book, you will realise that it constitutes an example of a kind of study technique. The chapters have been devised in the order in which you will encounter the various aspects of Shakespeare studies. We start with genre, setting and structure. We then move through characterisation to the more difficult areas of text, performance, culture and criticism. There is also a separate chapter on the poems. This organisation is deliberate. It mirrors a recommended way of coming to grips with these texts. In a sense it provides you with a working model of how to study at this level. Each chapter includes study notes and ideas that relate specifically to the chapter in which they appear. But the book as a whole also builds up to a comprehensive methodology.

The reason for this is simple. As mentioned previously, the way you organise your time and energy is crucial. Begin your study of a Shakespeare play with the basics, perhaps using some of the tips you will find in this book. This way, you will be adopting a rational approach to Shakespeare studies. You should define elements of the plays that are already familiar to you from previous encounters with the texts. You may start with genre, setting, plot and character, but these are not enough. Any university course will expect you to refine your awareness of these aspects of a play. You will begin to integrate them with the more difficult areas of performance, history and culture. In effect, you will use textual information to construct a basis for an argument. This is what a good piece of assessed work should do.

Most students will be taking a first-year course that does not concentrate on the Renaissance. If you are one of these, you will not be expected to be able to use a great deal of secondary material in the form of literary history or criticism. However, you should at least be aware of the major ideas and areas of interest. Many of these will be covered during your lecture schedule. You will probably not have the time to research every single essay in exactly the way you would like. Even so, if you are able to include some secondary works you will put yourself in a good position. The same goes for performance material. You may be able to get hold of some videos of performances; you may already own some. By paying attention to the dynamic nature of these texts as plays, you will also be helping yourself.

Unless you are taking a course specialism in drama, performance will not be a major part of your studies at this level. Most course structures are simply not able to allocate enough time to performance. Paradoxically, therefore, most of the time you will be dealing with Shakespeare's plays as reading texts. You should take every chance that comes your way to develop your awareness and knowledge of these texts as plays. Incidentally, all of these comments apply even more forcefully to a course of study that concentrates on the Renaissance period. They can be applied to higher-level, more intensive courses as well.

How to Proceed

You will probably have realised by now what is happening here. You are being asked to inter-relate the various ideas proposed in this book, and then to expand on that basis. The issues raised here will be presented to you in a pseudo-tutorial format. On most courses, you will be lucky to get one tutorial per week. If your course is not one that concentrates on the Renaissance, this means that you will be fortunate to get more than a single seminar session on Shakespeare. One of the things that this book seeks to do is to ensure that you get the most out of the possibilities open to you.

If you apply the ideas found in this volume, you will already be well on the way to making sensible decisions about how much time and effort you can afford to put into Shakespeare studies. If you are a student entering higher education for the first time, you need this kind of control.

1 Dealing with Genre

One-minute overview

A good starting point when studying Shakespeare's plays is genre, the way in which they are grouped. This basic classification gives you a context in which to work with the individual plays. Therefore, you will be able to appreciate that the comedies share certain characteristics that are different from, say, the tragedies. You will also find some pointers on Shakespeare's techniques in the different genres. These will include some comments on comedy and marriage; tragedy, character and society; dramatic rewriting of history and the balance of forces used to produce mixed-genre plays.

In this chapter we will be looking at:
- The comedies
- The tragedies
- The histories
- Mixed-genre plays

Comedies	Tragedies	Histories	Mixed Genre
The Comedy of Errors (1592–94)	Titus Andronicus (1593–94)	Henry VI Part 1 (1589–90)	Much Ado About Nothing (1598–99)
The Taming of the Shrew (1593–94)	Romeo and Juliet (1595–96)	Henry VI Part 2 (1590–91)	Troilus and Cressida (1601–02)
The Two Gentlemen of Verona (1594)	Julius Caesar (1599)	Henry VI Part 3 (1590–91)	All's Well That Ends Well (1602–03)

Fig. 1:
Table of Shakespeare's plays according to genre

Comedies	Tragedies	Histories	Mixed Genre
Love's Labour's Lost (1594–95)	Hamlet (1600–01)	Richard III (1592–93)	Measure For Measure (1604)
A Midsummer Night's Dream (1595–96)	Othello (1604)	King John (1594–96)	Pericles (1607–08)
The Merchant of Venice (1596–97)	King Lear (1605)	Richard II (1595)	Cymbeline (1609–10)
The Merry Wives of Windsor (1597)	Macbeth (1606)	Henry IV Part 1 (1596–97)	The Winter's Tale (1609–10)
As You Like It (1599)	Antony and Cleopatra (1606–07)	Henry IV Part 2 (1598)	The Tempest (1611)
Twelfth Night (1601–02)	Coriolanus (1607–08)	Henry V (1599)	The Two Noble Kinsmen (1613)
	Timon of Athens (1607–08)	Henry VIII (1612–13)	

Fig. 1:
Table of Shakespeare's plays according to genre (*cont'd*)

This table divides the plays into the four categories we will be discussing in this chapter. There are two things to note. The first is that many plays set in classical history and mythology are tragedies. The second is that the group of mixed-genre plays includes the so-called 'romances'.

The Comedies

Shakespeare's comedies were supposed to be funny, and all the evidence suggests that they were popular during his lifetime. However, even the tragedies have funny moments, so rather than define the comedies in terms of humour, critics do so through marriage. A good rule of thumb is, therefore, that a Shakespeare comedy will end in one or more marriages.

The events that occur during the course of a comedy will not necessarily be pleasant. In order to attain the aim of marriage, the heroes and heroines will first have to pass through various troubles. These must be overcome in order for the marriage resolution to take place. Shakespeare uses many different types of plot device to place obstructions in the way of lovers. Examples include supernatural intervention, for example the love juice in *A Midsummer Night's Dream*. There are commands from beyond the grave, as in the casket plot of *The Merchant of Venice*. And there are rivals in love, such as the suitors for Bianca's hand in *The Taming of the Shrew*.

Also, you must remember that these are plays, and one of the things Shakespeare often does is to take advantage of his audience's expectations. For example, he might use information unknown to his audience to help bring about a play's resolution. This is something he does when he introduces Mariana in *Measure for Measure* (IV.i). He also uses outright sleight of hand to achieve his aims, one famous example being the unrealistic bed trick from the same play. Several standard dramatic techniques that you will be asked to study in the comedies will be disguise, twins, mistakes and combinations of these.

The Tragedies

One way of looking at Shakespeare's tragedies is that they deal with the same issues as the comedies, but end in the deaths of the main characters and usually many others as well. Most critics have emphasised the importance of characterisation in these plays, although more recently a great deal of attention has been paid to social issues. You will probably be introduced to these problems as part of your course of study. You may believe that Macbeth is evil, for example, and you may continue to believe so after you have studied the play in more depth. Nevertheless, the single best piece of advice is that you should never take issues such as Macbeth's evil for granted. Do not assume that standard associations will be enough. You may be convinced that you are right and that everyone agrees with you. But as a student you must back up your assertions with evidence, either from the texts or from secondary reading. This is true of the other genres as well, but it is a particularly common problem with the tragedies.

Tragedy has often been taken as dependent on some moral flaw in the main character, or protagonist. This position is based upon Aristotle's views on the nature of tragedy. However, classical scholars have always maintained that Aristotle's term for the flaw, *hamartia*, is much more complex than a simple character flaw. Some Shakespeare critics are beginning to agree. Their argument is that *hamartia* refers to a flawed choice – a mistaken action. They argue that the tragedies are more about the social consequences of that action than about the main protagonists. According to these critics, our modern assumptions about the primacy of individual experience have blinded us. We have imposed on these old texts a whole series of incorrect associations. You will find more about these issues in Chapter 8; for the moment, remember that you will have to argue for any position you take.

As you will have seen from Fig. 1, five of the ten plays defined as tragedies take place in settings from classical history or mythology. This is because Shakespeare's contemporaries thought of plays such as *Antony and Cleopatra* as tragedies. In fact, this is how the play is listed in the *First Folio*, the first reasonably complete edition of the plays. Some critics treat these plays as a sub-group in their own right. However, you need to be careful here: even these so-called 'Roman plays' have Renaissance overtones, including anachronisms such as the chiming of a clock in *Julius Caesar* (II.i). It is important to remember that the term 'tragedy' refers not only to *Macbeth, King Lear, Hamlet* and *Othello*.

The plays set in the classical periods very often display a concern with anxieties that were close to home. Shakespeare and his contemporaries often set their plays in foreign or historical settings in order to address sensitive problems. By moving the plays elsewhere, the playwrights were able to dramatise contemporary issues while avoiding political censure. This technique is called displacement, and it often comes up in examinations and essays. One could argue that it is no coincidence that Shakespeare wrote *Julius Caesar* towards the end of the reign of Queen Elizabeth I. Worries about the succession abounded, especially since the official heir to the English throne was from another country – the King of Scotland, James VI. The death of the childless Caesar could be a commentary on the problems of Elizabeth's own childlessness. A play directly addressing the issue would have attracted the attention of the state censor, the Master of the Revels, who had jurisdiction over play texts. Therefore the playwright shifted the question to the career of a famous Roman.

The same could be said of the other tragedies. For example, you might not be surprised that *King Lear* was written just about the time of the change in monarchy from Queen Elizabeth I to James I. That play's concern with succession is certainly very contemporary. The Scottish play, *Macbeth*, also has very specific resonances with James' own interests. If you follow conventional critics and concentrate only on the main characters, you could be doing yourself – and the plays – a disservice.

The Histories

All of Shakespeare's plays were based on ideas by other people, or were drawn from historical events. He then played around with them, adding to them and changing some of the events he read about elsewhere. This is especially true of the history plays. You will not usually be asked too much about the sources of his material, but be very careful when you are claiming that some plot element or another is the invention of Shakespeare's imagination. You could be wrong.

The question of Shakespeare's intentions is therefore especially acute in relation to the English history plays. Apart from *King John* and *Henry VIII*, they are known as the two tetralogies, or sets of four. The First Tetralogy comprises the three parts of *Henry VI* plus *Richard III*. The Second Tetralogy is composed of *Richard II*, the two parts of *Henry IV* and *Henry V*. This can be very confusing, since it is based on the order in which the plays were written and performed, not their historical chronological order. Shakespeare wrote these plays during the reign of Queen Elizabeth I, of the

House of Tudor. Her family came to the throne at the end of the Wars of the Roses, so much of the material Shakespeare deals with in these plays is politically sensitive. Some critics go so far as to argue that he is effectively writing propaganda and that these plays represent the Tudors rewriting history. Assessment questions often draw upon this issue.

You must be very careful with the events you find in Shakespeare's histories. He often changed the emphases of historical events for dramatic purposes. For example, before the Battle of Agincourt, Henry V attempted to come to a peace agreement with the French. In Shakespeare's play, this is altered. During the night before the battle he does act secretly, but only to see how his men are bearing up (IV.i.88ff). The peace offer is relegated to a couple of exchanges with the herald of the French army (III.vi) and (IV.iii).

Another technique Shakespeare used a great deal was that of telescoping time. In *Richard III*, the good Duke Clarence is killed in the Tower of London because of his brother, who later becomes King Richard III(I.iv). On hearing the news of this death, the third brother, King Edward IV, has an apopleptic seizure from which he does not recover (II.i.80ff). In historical terms, this is complete nonsense. Clarence was executed in 1478, on Edward's orders, because he had been caught trying to commit treason against his elder brother for the third time. This was too much even for Edward. Incidentally, Edward died in 1483, five years after Clarence's death. Shakespeare has obviously rewritten this history in order to speed up events and focus the audience's interest on the figure of Richard.

Mixed-genre Plays

Many of Shakespeare's plays do not fit easily into the classifications explored above. For some critics, the events that take place in plays such as *Measure For Measure, Troilus And Cressida, All's Well That Ends Well, Much Ado About Nothing* and *The Merchant Of Venice* are so unpleasant that they seem to need another grouping altogether. This is why some of these have become known as the 'problem plays'. For example, although *Measure For Measure* may technically be a comedy because of the marriages arranged at the end of the play, the events that lead to those marriages make the play darker than, for example, *As You Like It*.

The critics do not necessarily agree on which plays should be treated in this way, and this gives examiners plenty of scope for essay questions. Be prepared for assessment titles such as 'Is *The Merchant of Venice* really a comedy?'. The one thing you can be sure of, however, is that Shakespeare was not alone in writing plays that were a mixture of dark and light or, if you prefer, tragedy and comedy. Around the beginning of the 17th century there was something of a vogue for plays that pushed against accepted norms. Audiences expected to be challenged and the playwrights produced dramas that drew upon elements of various genres. These are often called tragi-comedies, and the outcome is never certain until the very end of the play. Be sure to mention the historical context when you are dealing with plays by Shakespeare that might fall into this category.

The other mixed-genre plays are the so-called 'Romances': *Pericles, The Winter's Tale, The Tempest, The Two Noble Kinsmen* and *Cymbeline*. They are sometimes taken as a group because they exhibit certain fanciful features. They incorporate classical elements, magic and travel. They use plot lines that seem to link them, superficially at least, to a long tradition of tales of this nature. However, you must be extremely careful when employing the term 'Romance'. In relation to English literary history, it means many different things. It can refer to medieval romance poetry, with its heroes, tribulations and fair princesses. It is also a term used in relation to the Romantic poets of the late-18th and early-19th centuries. And then there are our modern conceptions of romance as sweet love. Shakespeare's plays pick up on aspects of the first of these categories: be sure not to get them mixed up with the others.

Tutorial

Study tips

1 Compare different editions of the *Complete Works of Shakespeare* to see how they classify the mixed-genre plays. Differences between them will alert you to possibilities for assessments.

2 Using the table of Shakespeare's plays provided (Fig. 1), work out which types of plays were written in which years. Are there periods in which he seemed to concentrate on certain kinds of plays? If so, why do you think he changed his interests?

Discussion points

1 Should Shakespeare's tragedies be analysed in terms of their protagonists? Or should social issues be taken into consideration as well?

2 At what point can we say that a comedy contains so many serious elements that it is more correct to define it as a mixed-genre play?

3 Categorise elements that seem to be common to Shakespearean comedy. Which of these are most important for which plays, and why?

Practical assignments

1 Look at past papers for your course or other similar courses. These will give you an idea of the kinds of questions that can come up in your assignments.

2 Take gender as a category. Shakespeare's plays often contain strong heroines; do the various genres use these female characters in the same way, or does their treatment vary depending on the kind of play they are in?

3 Decide on an important social issue, such as class mobility. Is this problem treated in the same way across generic boundaries, or are there substantial variations?

Practice questions

1 Shakespeare's comic heroines almost always end up getting married, no matter how powerful they might be in the course of a play. Is this a weakness in Shakespeare's plays?

2 Is the tragic protagonist always solely responsible for the chaos that erupts?

3 Is Shakespeare's treatment of important historical issues biased?

4 Is the category of 'mixed-genre plays' a helpful classification?

2 **Setting the Scene**

One-minute overview

You will remember from Chapter 1 that Shakespeare uses different techniques for the settings of his plays. In Chapter 2 we will see how he sometimes takes advantage of foreign locales in order to be free to dramatise sensitive issues. Even when he uses English history, he rearranges events to fit his theatrical treatment. In this chapter we will look at settings more closely, following on from the logic of genre. We will subdivide the settings of the plays as follows:

- The British Isles
- Late medieval and Renaissance Europe
- Classical history and mythology
- Somewhere else, some other time

Britain	Europe	Classical	Other
The Merry Wives of Windsor	The Taming of the Shrew	The Comedy of Errors	As You Like It
King Lear	The Two Gentlemen of Verona	A Midsummer Night's Dream	The Winter's Tale
Macbeth	Love's Labour's Lost	Troilus and Cressida	The Tempest
Cymbeline	The Merchant of Venice	Titus Andronicus	
Henry VI Part 1	Much Ado About Nothing	Julius Caesar	
Henry VI Part 2	Twelfth Night	Antony and Cleopatra	

Fig. 2:
Table of
Shakespeare's
plays according
to setting

Britain	Europe	Classical	Other
Henry VI Part 3	All's Well That Ends Well	Coriolanus	
Richard III	Measure For Measure	Timon of Athens	
King John	Romeo and Juliet	Pericles	
Richard II	Hamlet	The Two Noble Kinsmen	
Henry IV Part 1	Othello		
Henry IV Part 2			
Henry V			
Henry VIII			

▲
Fig. 2:
Table of
Shakespeare's
plays according
to setting
(*cont'd*)

This table gives you a breakdown of the locations of Shakespeare's plays. You will immediately see that very few of them are set in 'other' locations. This means that most of the plays are set in well-known contemporary or historical places. However, you must remember that these are Renaissance English versions of those places: they are not always what we would consider accurate or even reliable. Again, it should be stressed that these places are used and changed by Shakespeare for the purposes of dramatic action.

The British Isles

Shakespeare's English history plays are obviously almost entirely set in Britain, with the sole exception of *Henry V*, much of which takes place in France. However, only four other plays take place in the British Isles: *The Merry Wives of Windsor*, *Cymbeline*, *Macbeth* and *King Lear*.

The first of these cashes in on the popularity of the character of Falstaff from the *Henry IV* plays, and is unusual for Shakespeare in that it is set in middle-class English society. A persistent legend is that Queen Elizabeth I was so delighted by the creation of Falstaff that she commanded Shakespeare to give the character a starring role in his own comedy.

The other three are all set in semi-historical, semi-mythical periods in British history. This is a direct result of confusion in Shakespeare's source material. *Cymbeline* purports to be set in the time of the Roman Emperor Augustus. It shows the native British defeating Roman legions in combat, but its historical details are extremely suspect, to say the least. The same is true of the pseudo-Celtic Britain of *King Lear*. It includes recognisable titles such as Earl and Duke, a visiting King of France and a Duke of Burgundy. And, as any Scot will tell you, the history of *Macbeth* is simply wrong, although they might not be able to give you any specifics. But pure historical accuracy was not Shakespeare's aim; he wrote drama, and fiddling around with source material was an accepted, indeed praised, practice for Renaissance writers.

All of this means that Shakespeare was able to mix the contemporary problems that interested him with unusual settings. The technique allowed him to create a whole series of new linkages and meanings. It also let him play around with the locations, which would have been quite exotic to an English Renaissance audience. This logic of composition allowed the playwright to include other elements. One example is the witches in *Macbeth*. Their inclusion not only picks up on the strangeness of medieval Scottish history, but links them into the play's central concerns. In terms of the technique of displacement defined in Chapter 1, it allowed Shakespeare to refer safely to the new King's interest in witch cults. James VI of Scotland, who had become James I of England, had been heavily involved in witch investigations in Scotland before succeeding to the English throne.

Displacement therefore operates in time, as well as geographical setting. Problems of crucial political importance to Renaissance England could be addressed in a British setting sufficiently far from Shakespeare's own time. This was an important consideration in a time of state censorship. Thus, *Cymbeline* deals with Britain as heir to the Roman Empire. *Macbeth* explores the logic of a state that needs powerfully violent subjects for its own security – and the dangers when those subjects get out of hand. And *King Lear* investigates what happens when the ruler has no direct male heirs, a situation closely analogous to the succession problems of the Tudors.

Of course, Renaissance dramatists had to be especially careful with England's own political history. The nervousness of monarchs is exemplified by Queen Elizabeth I's reaction to the news that Shakespeare's *Richard II* had been revived at the moment of Essex's rebellion in 1601. The playwrights developed ways of managing the meanings that could be taken from a history play. They did this by ensuring that the historical events themselves were subordinated to dramatic concerns. First and foremost, these are populist recountings of history for the purposes of making money in the public theatres. As we have already seen with *Richard III*, techniques exist to help with this problem. The play might telescope time, emphasise certain events, leave out others and conflate several events into one. Another possibility is to associate an alternative view of history with a discredited faction such as the Yorkists. These methods were all used by Shakespeare at one point or another in his English history plays. Sometimes they are called 'chronicle' plays as a result, since medieval chronicles were not always particularly reliable.

Late Medieval and Renaissance Europe

Shakespeare came across the stories that were the basis for many of his plays in books on late medieval or Renaissance European history. He tended to elaborate upon a main single story and then integrate it with others. This is of course important for structure, which we will be looking at in the next chapter, but it also has implications for setting. What was it about continental Europe that attracted this dramatist?

Firstly, it is striking that most of the plays set in Europe are comedies. Secondly, the locations used are mostly, but not always, Italian. This is no coincidence: the Renaissance began in Italy, and many of the sources available to Shakespeare were English translations of Italian stories. Italian politics fascinated the English, giving rise in the plays of Christopher Marlowe to a composite villain figure known as the 'Machiavel'. He is the stage version of the political theorist

Machiavelli. Shakespeare picks up on such associations and integrates them into his own plays.

Religion is crucial here. Roman Catholic Italy was, at least in the view of some radical Protestants, totally corrupt. The actions of the medieval papacy did nothing to dispel this image, and indeed encouraged it in the eyes of the Protestants. The viciousness of the wars of religion unleashed by the Reformation and Counter-reformation did not quite reach England. For example, the British Isles remained largely untouched by the Thirty Years' War, (1618–48). This permitted the English to concentrate on their own affairs. However, at the time Shakespeare was writing, the attempted invasion of England by the Spanish Armada was still a vivid memory, and of course there were serious religious undertones to this conflict. The powerful Catholic monarchies of Spain and France, together with Italy, were fertile ground for all sorts of assumptions about foreigners when translated to the English stage.

Given this cultural context, even many of the comedies set in Europe have a dark side. A good example is the treatment of Shylock in *The Merchant of Venice*. Of course, not all of the comedies are like this. Many are simply set in the countries and cities Shakespeare found in his source material. Some, like *The Taming of the Shrew*, would probably not suffer from being shifted to England. When dealing with these plays, decide for yourself how important the setting is. You may consider that the courtly world of *Love's Labour's Lost* is much more important than the country in which it takes place. You may feel that other aspects of the plays merit more attention than the setting. Whatever you do, be prepared to argue for your choices.

Classical History and Mythology

These are sometimes misleadingly called 'Roman' plays. They are not all set in the context of ancient Roman history. *Coriolanus, Julius Caesar, Antony and Cleopatra* and *Titus Andronicus* are, but *Timon of Athens, Troilus and Cressida,*

Pericles, A Midsummer Night's Dream, The Comedy of Errors and *The Two Noble Kinsmen* are not. The easiest way to remember which is to realise that the plays set in Rome have some foundation in historical sources, while the others do not. Think of the Roman plays as historical, and the others as mythological (although *Timon of Athens* is set in a version of historical ancient Athens).

Julius Caesar and *Antony and Cleopatra* are often taken together as a logical pairing. The events associated with their storylines are well known, since they deal with the end of the Roman Republic and the rise of the Empire. *Titus Andronicus* is set in the late Empire, at a period when Rome was becoming increasingly reliant on outside help to try to maintain stable borders. *Coriolanus* is set at the beginning of Roman history, when the structures of the Republic were being worked out, usually violently. Both of these latter plays are tragedies, and it is interesting that *Titus Andronicus* was the first tragedy Shakespeare wrote, and *Coriolanus* the last. What was it about Roman history that drew Shakespeare back to it time and time again?

One answer to this question might be that all these plays deal with tumultuous events that see massive changes taking place in the state. They are concerned with the beginnings of Rome, the shift from Republic to Empire and then the disintegration of that Empire. Britain was itself on the way to becoming a major empire at the time Shakespeare was writing. So it may be no coincidence that the imagination of the popular theatre-going public in London was excited by the history of what had until then been the greatest empire known to western history.

As with the plays set in semi-historical Britain, Shakespeare gained great freedom by using Greek mythology. The context of classical legend allowed him to mix in various elements and enrich the theatrical experience for his customers. For example, *Timon of Athens* includes many of the conventions of Renaissance revenge drama, which at first sight may seem strange in a classical play. But of course Renaissance drama is itself heavily indebted to the plays of the Roman writer Seneca, which are just as sensationalist.

Such mixtures are common to all of the plays we are looking at in this section. A *Midsummer Night's Dream* is set in mythological Athens. But it also incorporates elements of Renaissance English country folklore and a parody of the working city artisans who watched plays by Shakespeare and his contemporaries. *The Two Noble Kinsmen*, which was written in collaboration with another major dramatist, John Fletcher, returns to this same Athens, but dramatises the chivalric code of Chaucer's *Knight's Tale*. *Troilus and Cressida* picks up on another story used by Chaucer, in the setting of the Trojan War. And *Pericles* is a kind of *Odyssey*, with the hero undergoing troubles and voyages before he finally finds fulfilment. All of these plays operate in a kind of mixed mode, with elements of different traditions appearing when the playwright finds them useful.

Somewhere Else, Some Other Time

Although *As You Like It* is set in a forest named Arden in an unspecified country, *The Tempest* is the play that most obviously takes place in an uncertain location. The island that has been colonised by Prospero is probably somewhere between Milan and Tunis, but it is left undefined. This allowed Shakespeare to include various extra meanings that would not be possible if the play were set in a well-known area. Most editions of the play link it with a famous expedition to the Bermudas. The figure of Caliban is on the island before the arrival of Prospero and Miranda. In addition, magical islands were common in Greek mythology, and this play echoes the power of sorceresses such as Circe. All of these associations make the time period of the play seem somewhat nebulous. This is true also of *The Winter's Tale*, which contains a prophecy from Apollo. But part of its action takes place in Bohemia, which is hardly a classical location.

The fact that Shakespeare gives Bohemia a coast is a famous mistake on his part. However, it also points to a certain logic in his dramatic works: he is not interested in geographical or historical accuracy. The point is that history, geography and mythology can all be used in the settings of the plays, but are subordinate to dramatic concerns. This is extremely important. It means that even plays which seem straightforward in setting are actually more complex on further investigation. *Hamlet* and *Macbeth* are set in medieval times, in Denmark and Scotland respectively. However, these are English Renaissance versions of those historical and geographical locations. The ways in which Shakespeare uses them to address issues of concern to his contemporary audience are much more important to the plays as drama.

Tutorial

Study tips

1. As you go through a play scene by scene, make a list of the moments when the setting shifts. Depending on the play, you will be able to find a complex criss-crossing of locations that mirrors important plot elements. If several of these locations keep cropping up, you will be able to see how Shakespeare integrates dynamic action and setting.

2. If a play is pretty much set in one area, use the technique suggested above to see how the action is divided up between various individuals in the play. The variations you will find are the dramatist's way of introducing subtle movement into what seems to be a static environment.

Discussion points

1. Plays such as *Richard III* include alternative versions of English history. Trace out the points when these alternatives are given, and discuss their implications for the 'official' version.

2. Most editions of single plays will include some material on Shakespeare's sources. Work out the ways in which he incorporated this information; what does this tell you about the way he used the sources for the basis of dramatic presentations?

3 Take a play that has a specific historical setting Discuss how you would take advantage of images from this period as an important visual element of a production.

4 Decide on a play that has multiple shifts of action and setting, such as *Pericles*. Discuss how you would make each of the shifts make sense to an audience, utilising costume, stage scenery, gesture, etc.

Practical assignments

1 When a play relies on very few locations for its action, you need to make each location contain visual elements that strongly identify it for the audience. If you were directing such a play, how would you accomplish this? Go to a library that gives you access to videos and photographs of the plays to see how they deal with this problem.

2 Decide on a play that deals with important political events. Group the various scenes that relate to one of the factions involved in the political action. Work out which theatrical techniques you would use to make this faction easily identifiable to a modern audience. Search for visual materials associated with the period and location of your chosen play and decide how these could be used as part of a production.

Practice questions

1 How does a Shakespearean play update historical elements in order to make them understandable to a Renaissance audience?

2 In what ways do Shakespeare's plays take advantage of their setting in time and place to deal with sensitive political and/or social issues?

3 Describe how Shakespeare manages scene changes to illustrate differences between various locations in his plays.

3 Untangling the Structure

One-minute overview

Students who have come across Shakespeare's plays before may be expecting the emphasis of this chapter to be on plot. However, the concept of plotting owes more to the novel than to drama. The term 'structure' is preferred at more advanced levels of study and when you are asked to write about it you should try to develop some idea of how to relate it to performance issues. Shakespeare's plays use various forms of structure to underpin the dramatic action. As the backbone of a play, the structure will have crucial implications for the way in which the play's action evolves.

In this chapter we shall be looking at:
- The main storyline
- Double structure one: subplot
- Double structure two: interspersing
- Double structure three: chiasmus
- Dynamic structures

The Main Storyline

The idea of a play having a main storyline is an obvious but misleading one. The problem is that it refers to the events of the play as though they were a single straightforward narrative, which of course is never the case. It also leaves out the crucial terrain of the stage itself – the performance. Nevertheless, it is a useful enabling concept, a tool for further analysis.

Very few of Shakespeare's plays have only a single main storyline. Even a relatively short play such as *Macbeth*, with its concentration on the central figure's rise and fall, contains other aspects as well. There is the play's insistence, at least for the first half, on the importance of Lady Macbeth. There are also the scenes with the witches and an important scene set in England. Other plays are even more complex, and we will be dealing with them later. For the moment, a good starting point is to look at how plays with an obvious major plot line link in with genre and setting, which we have already discussed. This will provide us with a useful beginning.

If you have been following this book in the recommended chapter order, you will already have a good idea of how genre and setting operate. In particular, you should be aware of how they can be integrated into an overall whole. In other words, you are beginning to lay the foundation for a thorough analysis. In this you are not alone: it is a common baseline rehearsal technique.

Let us continue with the example of *Macbeth*. It is of course a tragedy, although there is at least one humorous part in it, that of the gatekeeper. This immediately tells you one thing: if this is a tragedy, then you don't want too much comedy. Unfortunately, comedy has a way of arising unexpectedly. The witches are especially problematic here. For a modern audience these are simply unrealistic, and the first appearance of the witches can make a production descend into farce. As a student, you will be able to manipulate this. For example, you could be asked to write an essay that in some way includes an evaluation of the role of the witches. A good way to do this would be to start from a realisation that they can pose a problem. You would then proceed to an analysis of the kinds of meanings they might have had for a contemporary Renaissance audience. In this way you pay attention to two important issues: performance and historical context.

The implications of setting can now be included in your essay. If you want to explore how the witches might be most effective, you have two choices. One is to describe how they might have been played in the Renaissance open-air theatres (see Chapter 6); the other is to deal with how they could be updated, either on stage or on film. You are already making decisions here about the setting in which the witches appear. Additionally, the play sets up major differences between the court of King Duncan and that of the Macbeths. Does this mean that you see the play as posing three major setting possibilities: the realm of good King Duncan, the realm of Macbeth, and the witches somewhere in the middle?

If so, then you are already beginning to come to terms with the main storyline of the play. But you are not doing so in any simplistic manner. Instead, you are paying a great deal of attention to how the play moves the action forward from the world of Duncan to that of Macbeth, via the witches. In fact, many productions have used shifts in the setting as the basis for decisions about the visual aspects of the play. You could be justified in thinking of Duncan's court as very similar to that of medieval England, while Macbeth's is more that of a highland chief. These are not historically accurate differentiations, but they are highly symbolic. And then what do you do with the witches? In order to underline their symbiosis with Macbeth, do you make them into some kind of Celtic wise women?

Double Structure One: Subplot

You will probably have come across the concept of a subplot in Shakespearean drama. However, the logic of double structure is much more far reaching in its implications. The subplot is the simplest version of the double structure. In plays such as King Lear, a secondary plot is set in motion which comments on and sheds light upon the main storyline. The minor story is linked to the main part of the play by the character of Edmund. The term 'subplot' automatically implies that one strand of the play's events is subordinate to the other.

There are plays for which the concept of subplot is inadequate. In *The Merchant of Venice*, the two stories of Shylock and Bassanio are kept separate for much of the play. Unlike the secondary elements of *King Lear*, it is not until quite late in the play that they are brought together – and then only in the person of Portia, disguised as a young lawyer. Shylock is vanquished and the play moves on to what many have considered to be a rather insipid fifth act.

Do you remember the caution expressed in the previous chapter about a modern audience's reception of the witches in *Macbeth*? If so, then you should also be alert to a similar problem here in *The Merchant of Venice*. What is it about the fifth act that makes it seem so poor by comparison with what goes before? Is it because the play on the language and meaning of love seem less exciting than the trial scene? If this is so, then why did Shakespeare spend so much time, indeed the play's resolution, on a far less interesting aspect of the play as a whole?

As with the witches, the problem may not be with the play, but with changing perceptions of its significance. *The Merchant of Venice* has a very tightly woven double structure; if later audiences and readers find the final act boring, does it necessarily follow that Shakespeare's contemporaries also did? Many other plays from the period are deeply concerned with the meaning of truth and language in love. In the Belmont plot line of this play, the significance of rings and promises is highlighted. It might be that the modern reception of the play has problems precisely because of the double structure: Shylock simply seems much more important. This is hardly surprising given the experiences of 20th-century history, but it is something that has been developing for longer than this. For many years, Shylock was considered one of the great parts that every aspiring actor should play. Why was this the case?

If you are taking other courses in literary studies, now is your chance to integrate those studies with your work on Shakespeare. If you can link some of what you learn in one course with material from others, you will cut down on the effort required overall. You will probably not be able to answer on the same text in more than one course, but that does not prevent you from being able to make logical inferences. The Shylock situation just described is a good example of this technique. As with *Macbeth*, it could be argued that the root of the problem lies in changes in meaning. A single powerful character such as Shylock now seems much more interesting than a group of lovers. It is no coincidence that modern western society now tends to emphasise the importance of the individual at the expense of his or her place in society.

If you are also studying the development of the novel, or of poetry, you will see that the importance of individual experience increases radically the further away you move from the period of the Renaissance. This movement is accelerated by the Romantic poets, who place great emphasis on the power of the individual imagination. But Shakespeare's plays pre-date this phenomenon. Although you may feel that aspects of this historical movement can be detected in his works, the tendency is not yet so pronounced. The prime importance of the individual was not a major concern for Shakespeare. This is why he used double structures to include elements that seem rather weak to us.

Not all criticism of the plays takes this view. But remember the caution expressed at the beginning of Chapter 1. Critics who look for meaning only in the protagonists do so at the expense of other meanings. Chapter 8 will explore these problems more fully. For the moment, it is enough to realise that there are debates. You will not yet need to deal with them, but you do need to be aware that they exist. Ultimately, what matters is how *you* view the plays. If you are going to use critical material to back up your viewpoint, you need to know enough about the critics to be able to make a choice.

Double Structure Two: Interspersing

The social world these plays construct is far too complex for other meanings to be ignored. This explains the importance of the double structure: it forces the audience to pay more attention to multiple segments of the drama. The implications of the double structure for the dynamics of performance should not be underestimated. The logic of the subplot should be remembered here. In some plays one part can be subordinated to another as a kind of running commentary. But what happens in a play with a more fully evolved double structure? Both parts are equally important and so the rounded social world of the play is more fully explored. A good example of this structure can be found in the first part of *Henry IV*. The following diagram divides this play into two strands. The first and most obvious is the 'heroic' level of great historical deeds. The second, which has been highlighted in bold type, undercuts that level.

As you can see, this play is divided almost equally between the two parts of the double structure. But unlike *The Merchant of Venice*, in this play the action is not set in two different places. Rather, the action of the Falstaff part of the play faithfully follows on from the political history of the kingdom.

You will note that the interspersing of the two major levels of the play is not symmetrical. This is because a straightforward alternation would be predictable, and would detract from the play's overall dynamism. Also, you should be aware that these are not Shakespeare's own scene divisions.

▶

Fig. 3:
The double
structure of
Henry IV part 1

I.i	The King's court.
I.ii	**Prince Henry, Falstaff and Poins.**
I.iii	The King's court: trouble brewing.
II.i	**The tavern.**
II.ii	**The Gadshill robbery.**
II.iii	The Hotspur household.
II.iv	**The tavern: double inversion of the Royal court.**
III.i	The conspirators.
III.ii	The Royal court. Interplay between King Henry and his son.
III.iii	**The tavern.**
IV.i	The conspirators.
IV.ii	**Falstaff and Bardolph.** Hal and Westmoreland appear.
IV.iii	The conspirators.
IV.iv	York; preparation for *Henry IV part 2*.
V.i	Parley. **Falstaff on honour.**
V.ii	The conspirators.
V.iii	First battle scene: Hotspur and Douglas. **Hal and Falstaff.**
V.iv	Second battle scene: Hotspur and Prince Hal. **Falstaff and Douglas.**
V.v	The aftermath.

They were interpolated by later editors. They have broken down the play into acts and scenes based on the distinctions they think are logical. The good thing about this from your point of view is that you already have a set of ready-made divisions.

Shakespeare's technique here is to make Falstaff's version of the war parallel that of the official history very closely. Falstaff and his friends constitute a very close sub-version of the heroic world that the nobles seek to inhabit. This means that the play is able to dramatise another, competing history. The ways in which the two versions move off against each other provides the structural dynamic for the play as a whole. And it is no accident that the two halves come together on stage with Falstaff's 'death' and the heroic single combat between Prince Hal and Percy.

Double Structure Three: Chiasmus

So far we have looked at two kinds of double structure. But there is a third, and it is even more dynamic than those we have seen so far. It is one that occurs in plays with binary pairings that do not so much progress together as swap over by the end of the play. For instance, in *The Taming of the Shrew* Petruchio's wooing of Kate is counterbalanced by Lucentio's attempt to marry Bianca. The play sets up the two sisters in opposition to each other: Kate is the shrew, while Bianca, as her name denotes, is pure and obedient. However, by the end of this play the two sisters have changed to diametrically opposite positions. Bianca now refuses to obey her husband, while Kate has become completely subjugated to hers. This criss-crossing structure is called 'chiasmus', after the Greek letter 'chi', or 'X'.

Chiasmus can work through location as well as characters. In *A Midsummer Night's Dream* the city of Athens is set up in opposition to the world of the fairies. Consequently, the nobility of Athens is contrasted with the fairy king and queen. These oppositions are dynamic and affect the way in which the four young Athenian nobles move from Athens to the woods and back again. Remember that Demetrius is the only one of the four youths who goes back to Athens permanently changed by his experiences. He remains under the influence of Oberon's drug.

In this play the wood is not the wildest location mentioned. There is an even wilder possibility, one that is discussed by Puck and Oberon (III.ii.378 – 388). It means that the wood is not only juxtaposed with Athens, but that it also occupies a sort of medium point between civilisation and total wilderness. The technical term for such a place is 'liminal space', from the Latin 'limen' meaning 'threshold, or doorway'. The ways in which the various characters move in and through this liminal space make the play extremely dynamic. The play is constructed around a liminal space and its relation, through chiasmus, to the city of Athens.

Dynamic Structures

Many Renaissance plays are structured in even more complex ways, and Shakespeare uses these techniques as well. *The Merry Wives of Windsor*, for example, has many characters plotting against one another, all at the same time. Even though the plot that is given the most attention is the fooling of Falstaff by Mrs Page and Mrs Ford, much energy is expended on the rest of the characters as well. The Welsh parson, Hugh Evans, and the French Doctor Caius both wish to be married to Anne Page, and attempt to fight a duel for her. The Host of the Garter Inn fools them both by keeping them apart; they then desire revenge upon him and plot together. At the same time, there are two other suitors for Anne's hand: Slender, cousin of the local Justice of the Peace, and a young gentleman named Fenton. Mrs Page favours Dr Caius as suitor, while her husband favours Slender. Anne herself prefers Fenton. And, at the same time as Falstaff is being fooled, Mr Ford suspects his wife of genuinely having an affair with Falstaff.

All of this is complex enough, but the play is in fact even more dynamic. The reason for this is that the characters change. Caius and Evans begin by trying to fight each other, but then become compatriots against the Host. Mr Ford joins in the plot to fool Falstaff after his wife proves innocent; he shifts from jealous husband to willing participant in her schemes. And, at the very end of the play, Anne's three different suitors all try to marry her secretly, but only Fenton succeeds.

To sum up: not only are there multiple simultaneous plots, but the participants change their roles as well. To a modern audience and, especially, a modern reader, these shifts and changes can be very confusing. But Renaissance audiences were used to the dynamic possibilities opened up by the public theatres. They were alert to the quick changes that to us seem difficult to follow. This is another important difference between Renaissance and modern perceptions. It may even help to explain why some of the plays are now performed more often than others.

Tutorial

Study tips

1 When you are studying the structure of a play, draw a diagram that groups characters according to the locations with which they are associated. You will very quickly develop a good idea of which characters are associated with specific elements of the plot, and how they move from one place to another. This is an extremely useful exercise when you have to study a play with many characters. It is also an excellent way of managing the history plays in particular, where the profusion of noble characters can be confusing.

2 If your group is studying a very dynamic play, assign one major part to each person in the group. Everyone should then discuss in turn how they see their part changing as the play progresses. This is a very useful way of dealing with a difficult play, since it divides up the study of the characters and how they interact with the structure. Sharing your workload like this may help you manage your study time more effectively.

Discussion points

1 Pick a play with a relatively straightforward structure. Discuss whether the few other sections should be cut altogether, or whether they help shed light on the main storyline.

2 Discuss why Shakespeare used different structures for different plays. Is a relatively clear-cut construction more suited to a specific genre like tragedy?

Practical assignments

1 Divide your study group into two and assign each half part of a play with a double structure. Ask each group to report on how they think their half of the play is constructed. Then discuss how the play relates to the various kinds of double structure you have come across in this chapter.

2 Go to a library or resource centre and borrow a CD-rom version of one or more Shakespeare plays. These tend to show one scene at a time on screen. Pick a play and read through it on screen. Because you have to load each scene separately, you will find yourself paying a great deal of attention to the way the play moves from scene to scene. This is an exceptionally simple and effective way of coming to grips with a play's structure.

Practice questions

1 Is there a point at which a play's structure becomes so complex that it constitutes a major problem?

2 How does Shakespeare integrate a play's action with its structure in a way that keeps the various characters clearly differentiated for the audience?

4 **Considering Character**

One-minute overview

Now is your chance to develop any prior ideas you may already have about characterisation. But characters in these plays do not stand alone. They are intimately related to a whole host of other characters, as well as the considerations of genre, setting and structure already described. Shakespeare's plays build upon character types already developed in previous periods of dramatic history. They also pick up on some new movements.

In this chapter, we will be meeting:
- Stock character types
- Heroes of tragedy and history
- Heroines of tragedy and history
- Men in the comedies
- Women in the comedies
- Other characters

Stock Character Types

First things first. Never start off from the assumption that any character in a Shakespeare play is a real, living person. You may think that their psychology, especially in performance, makes them seem realistic. But you have to argue for this position. Shakespeare's drama developed from a tradition of popular travelling players and interludes sponsored by city authorities in the midst of church celebrations. Much of the characterisation you will find in a Shakespeare play has to be seen in terms of an ongoing tradition.

The so-called 'stock' characters are important here. Following on from the history of popular performance, the plays are full of what we might think of as minor parts.

But for the playgoing public of the time, these easily identifiable types fulfilled important functions. They gave clues that linked the figures on the stage to events in the plot in an easily identifiable way.

The perspective afforded by reference to popular dramatic tradition throws up some other associations. At first sight, these may seem odd and rather startling. We are used to thinking of Shakespeare as high culture, but to his contemporaries these plays were first and foremost popular entertainment. The stock characters work within the same logic as those in modern pantomime. There is the fool, the unruly woman, the bad guy (they're usually male) and the topsy-turvy king. Such figures are easily recognisable in exactly the same way as the Principal Boy in a panto. In fact, it could be said that modern pantomime is a bastardised descendant of the popular dramatic stereotypes used by Shakespeare and his contemporaries.

Examples would be the fool in many of the comedies, as well as *King Lear*; Kate in *The Taming of the Shrew* or Beatrice in *Much Ado About Nothing*; Iago in *Othello*; and Lear in *King Lear*. These figures are all descended from the medieval carnival tradition and you must be aware of this when writing about them. Once again, do not simply assume that they are fully rounded personalities in the ways expected by some modern audiences.

The best way to demonstrate the problem is to look at one character in some detail. At different times in *Othello*, Iago gives completely contradictory reasons as to why he wants to destroy Othello. The first comes at the very beginning of the play, when he is encouraging Roderigo (I.i.8ff). Here he tries to reassure his confederate by recounting how Othello passed him over for promotion in favour of Cassio. He describes the latter as 'a great arithmetician … that never set a squadron in the field' (I.i.19–22). Just before the expedition to Cyprus, Iago gives a completely different justification. He tells the audience that he thinks his wife has been seeing Othello behind his back (I.iii.386–8). Following on from this, he decides that he loves Desdemona as well. He does this both in order to avenge himself on Othello and because he says he is attracted to Desdemona's beauty (II.i.291ff).

Iago gives three completely different reasons for his intention to destroy Othello. In terms of coherent character psychology, this makes no sense. But here the stock character of the medieval 'Vice' is being adapted to Renaissance stage requirements. Shakespeare is also picking up on the 'Machiavel' figure of Christopher Marlowe's plays. The result is a synthesis of tradition and new performance requirements. So there is a great deal more to a figure such as Iago than might at first be apparent. Modern assumptions about psychology tend to obscure these more complex associations.

Heroes of Tragedy and History

The above comments about Iago can also be applied to other characters, including the major protagonists. The performance requirements of the time had a long history and you will find out more about this in Chapter 7. For the moment, you should think about how an important character such as a main hero fits into the social world around him. This applies on two levels: the performance culture in general and the world constructed in the play.

For example, the figure of Lear operates in several ways. He is a topsy-turvy king in the tradition of popular performance. He is a monarch who lives within a social world. He gives his power away while attempting to retain its outward trappings. And he is driven insane by the realisation that to give away power is final: he becomes a subject. Simply to analyse such a complex situation in terms of character psychology may only scratch the surface.

The same can be said of Hamlet. You may think that his feelings of alienation and incapacity are very modern, and you would not be the first to say so. But notice his language: he lives in a world saturated with images of earth and land ownership. This marks him out as inhabiting a world that makes sense of itself through a vocabulary of the land. In other words, he uses the language of the feudal state, even as that state disintegrates all around him. Also, in contemporary emblem books, a young man dressed in black holding a skull stands for melancholy. The image we take for granted as signifying the pain of the individual meant something completely different to Shakespeare's audience.

The Renaissance is often taken as the starting point for the development of individualism. If you see echoes of this in Shakespeare's plays, you will have to argue for them. You may in fact see a tension between a new form of individual experience on the one hand and the older social forms on the other. Such a context could provide you with an insight into the world of figures such as Lear and Hamlet. They both try desperately to make sense of radical changes in their environment. Lear attempts to hang on to as much of the old social order as he possibly can. Yet he is the one who inaugurates that system's demise by relinquishing power to his daughters. Hamlet tries to make sense of massive changes in the state of Denmark, driven by the forbidden knowledge that his father was secretly murdered. And remember that even this knowledge comes from an apparition. Can it be trusted?

In a sense, the plays set up a tension between the hero, or protagonist, and upheavals in the social world. This explains the emergence of Goneril, Regan and Edmund in *King Lear*. They are concerned only with their own ruthless self interest. Similar characters can be found in the other plays: Claudius in *Hamlet*, for example. Sometimes the focus on their world view is so intense that a play uses one of these new politicians as a main character, such as *Richard III*. The ways in which the individual protagonist plays off against society in these histories and tragedies is extremely important. They may act powerfully and malevolently. They may be paralysed into inaction. Or they may be swept along by events beyond their control. Whatever the situation, the outcome is usually violent.

Heroines of Tragedy and History

The same goes for the women, only even more so. There is some debate about the possibilities open to women in this period. Certainly the throne was occupied by a very powerful queen for the first part of Shakespeare's output. But this does not necessarily translate into a better deal for all women. The situation probably varied according to how privileged the individual woman was. And, of course, society does not usually change overnight just because of one famous person. The technical term for a society structured to the advantage of men is patriarchy, and this includes Shakespeare's society.

Within this broad historical context, the patriarchal ideal was a beautiful chaste woman who remained silent. However, there are always exceptions – such as Queen Elizabeth I. Therefore, although the society was patriarchal, it was also aware that other possibilities could exist for women. Drama picks up very powerfully on such underlying social tensions, and Shakespeare's plays are no exception.

Some of the female characters in Shakespeare's histories and tragedies fit the patriarchal mould, for example Lady Anne in *Richard III*. One of the most important scenes in the play as far as performing Richard is concerned is the famous wooing scene in I.ii. This is an extreme example of the female character as pure passivity. She is accompanying the corpse of King Henry VI and meets Richard, who was also responsible for the death of her husband, Henry's son Edward. Even so, regardless of the damage he has done her, she ends up agreeing to marry him.

As far as Anne operates as an embodiment of gender roles, she is pretty much a straightforward stereotype, the passive woman. But if you remember the caution expressed earlier about Shakespeare's histories, a different story emerges. Anne was one of the daughters of the powerful Warwick, known as 'the kingmaker'. Warwick had originally supported the Yorkist faction to which Richard belonged. However, he betrayed them and betrothed Anne to Prince Edward of the House of Lancaster. His other daughter was married off to Clarence, Richard's brother. Warwick therefore played with both Royal families at different times. This is all very confusing, but one salient fact stands out: these women were the pawns of powerful nobles. Their availability for marriage was exploited as part of the normal course of politics. After the death of her first husband, she married Richard. Shakespeare takes all of this history, condenses it and dramatises it completely ahistorically as a single scene. The stereotypical passive woman becomes Richard the villain's ultimate victim: in a sense, one stock character meets another.

At first, Anne is vitriolic and violent towards Richard. This is crucially important, because it affords a glimpse of the opposite stereotype: the witch. For Renaissance patriarchy, if a woman does not act in accordance with the ideal of passivity, she must logically be its opposite. If you're not controlled, you must be well out of control.

The same is true of Goneril, Regan, Lady Macbeth and a host of others. The language they use about themselves accords with how the men who are their victims describe them. They seem unnatural, beastly and dangerous, especially in the secure power they have over their own sexuality. Edmund in *King Lear* is just as vicious towards his father as the two princesses are to Lear. But the most demonic language is used by Lear in relation to his daughters. This is a key description: the technical term for the extreme denigration of a powerful woman is 'demonisation'.

Lear decribes Cordelia in exactly the same way when she refuses to obey him. The play dramatises a conflict within Lear's patriarchy by putting Cordelia in an impossible position. She must obey her father. But she must also remain silent, as the embodiment of ideal femininity. You could argue that this lays bare the way in which the positions of demonic witch and ideal madonna are assigned to women by men. In other words, the play's action is dynamic.

There is, of course, one other position conventionally available to women: they can go mad. Ophelia is another female character who is given massively conflicting prerogatives. She must pass from her father to her future husband, in accordance with the laws of marriage. But she is being asked by her father to act as a spy upon Hamlet, in order to fit in with the new politics of Claudius' court. The resulting impasse is intolerable. And it is no coincidence that many of the active women in Shakespeare's plays have hints of this insanity, for example Queen Margaret in the *Henry VI* plays and *Richard III* and the deaths of Lady Macbeth, Goneril and Regan.

With the major female figures in the histories and tragedies you should adopt the same procedures as you do with the men. Compare the character's role to the play world within which they operate. And always remember the context of performance. Ask yourself how these personae work within the tradition of Renaissance public performance. That way you will avoid ascribing simplistic notions of psychology to them that would be more in keeping with someone in a 19th-century realist novel. This procedure will also help you to deal with more problematic figures such as Cleopatra. She does not seem to fit easily into any of the standard categories discussed here. She upsets the stereotypes and moves dynamically between them. You need a set of tools that enables you to deal with such a situation. Treating these complex dramatic characters as though they were real people from a later age is not sufficient.

Men in the Comedies

These come in three broad categories: chancers, wimps and the bad guys. Once again, these are in keeping with the dramatic tradition inherited by Shakespeare. There are of course others who do not quite fit into these categories, such as Benedick in *Much Ado About Nothing*. But in general, the stereotype is a good place to begin.

The wimps are easy to spot. They are men like Duke Orsino in *Twelfth Night* or Antonio in *The Merchant of Venice*. Their relative lack of dramatic impact is not simply a result of the fact that they are passive. If they act at all, they do so in response to someone else's initial activity. But the main reason for their colourlessness is to do with Renaissance ideas of psychology. In that period, psychology was thought of in terms of an ideal balance of humours within the body. If one humour, or fluid, is prevalent, then the person is mentally out of balance. Hamlet, as mentioned before, is a stereotype of melancholy based on this theory. Antonio complains often about being out of sorts and is unable to put his finger on the cause. In *Twelfth Night* Duke Orsino suffers from love melancholy. A modern audience might think of them as effeminate. But when you consider the historical context, it is their lack of activity that marks them out as having problems.

Although these characters are passive, they are crucial to the plays of which they are part. It is their relative lack of activity that allows the plot to be moved on. Orsino is so much in love with Olivia that he needs a go-between, and this is where Cesario/Viola comes in. Antonio provides the necessary link in *The Merchant of Venice* between the mercantile world of Venice and the aristocracy of Belmont. After all, it is his money that bankrolls Bassanio's courting of Portia.

This brings us to the chancers. Bassanio is one, of course, as is Petruchio in *The Taming of the Shrew*. Both are based on standard dramatic types. Bassanio is a common Renaissance figure, the impoverished gentleman who has squandered his fortune and needs to marry for money. Petruchio is straight out of the medieval carnival tradition. He is the fool, the one who takes great delight in inhabiting the topsy-turvy world of the festive holiday. His relationship with Kate exactly parallels that of Punch and Judy.

The bad guys also come from these important influences. But they often seem more rounded than those discussed so far. This may be because they are up against it, usually as outsiders, which makes them more interesting. Not all of them are like this, of course. There are figures such as Don John in *Much Ado About Nothing*. Although the consequences of his plotting are crucial, he himself has very little stage time.

There are also characters such as Shylock in *The Merchant of Venice* or Caliban in *The Tempest*. They are given the opportunity to explain the reasons for their hatred of the main characters. Certainly some later audiences have found some sympathy with them, but this is more a result of historical events subsequent to the Renaissance and changing perceptions. For a Renaissance audience, Shylock is just the bad guy. His persona is enhanced even further by the fact that he is a racial caricature.

Women in the Comedies

In the comedies, women are at least as active as they are in the tragedies, perhaps even more so. In the tragedies and histories, women are often constrained in what they can do. The society in which they move is very closely based on a Renaissance idea of what their world was like. This means that, since politics in those periods was very much the province of men, the women tend to fit into the categories discussed earlier.

But the world of comedy has other possibilities, some of which verge on the farcical. One very important element of many of these plays is an openness of opportunity for the female characters. A very common technique used here is that of disguise. In order to be able to act, the women successfully allow themselves to be taken for men. This can lead to an impasse, as in *Twelfth Night* or *As You Like It*. In both these plays the female lead is able to use disguise to get close to the man she loves. But that disguise then becomes a barrier to further contact.

There are many implications of the use of disguise. Remember that all of the parts in these plays were taken by male actors. Situations can arise in which a male playing the part of a woman is then further disguised as a man. There is a great deal of debate about how such drama might interrogate gender assumptions, or at least disclose how gender categories operate. You may feel that in many instances the Renaissance audience simply took it for granted that what was being represented on stage was a woman, and leave it at that. Or you may think that, on occasion, these issues are being exploited and even directly addressed. A good example would be Kate's epilogue to *The Taming of the Shrew*. Here a man plays the part of a woman who refuses to be controlled and is then browbeaten into marriage. 'She' then exhorts all of the women in the audience to obey their menfolk. In other words, a man dressed like a woman tells women to obey men.

The comedies provide many opportunities for women characters. It will be up to you to argue just how open this is. But again, it must be emphasised that you will have to be careful. Always back up your arguments with textual evidence. Many of these female figures work in exactly the same ways as the men in that they come out of a vibrant dramatic background.

Other Characters

Many minor characters flit in and out of the background of the plays. Sometimes they provide an important part of the plot line and sometimes they seem superfluous. However, you need to remember that what might seem unimportant now may not have been so to a Renaissance audience. Often these parts exist for comic relief as well as to comment on the action. The Porter in *Macbeth* and the gravediggers in *Hamlet* are good examples.

Sometimes there are other considerations. A good example can be found in *Julius Caesar* (III.iii). This is a scene that seems to make no sense. Cinna, a poet who happens to have the same name as one of the conspirators who killed Caesar, is himself killed by the mob. They are rioting after Antony's famous funeral oration. Even after he tells them that he is not the Cinna they are looking for, they kill him anyway. Remember the importance of names in this play in particular, and in Renaissance culture generally. This is a world in which name, lineage and dynasty are crucial, because they are markers of social position. The scene functions emblematically to draw the audience's attention to the play's overall concern – there will be more about this technique in Chapter 6. It also portrays mob violence at work, something that terrified late Elizabethan society. By the time *Julius Caesar* was written and performed, there had been a great deal of social unrest. The prime reasons for this were the enclosure by private landowners of land previously considered to be held in common, and a series of bad harvests. Shakespeare's play therefore demonstrates what can happen when anarchy rules.

Another example comes in *King Lear* (II.i). Here Edmund meets with a man named Curan, who is a minor courtier. His name is derived from the Latin verb *currere*, which means 'to run'. This is the root of English terms such as 'river current'. This scene might appear at first to be completely superfluous, since it does not advance the plot. But it does show the movement of courtiers and messengers behind the scenes in the new Britain of Goneril and Regan. The way royal business is conducted is therefore more secret than the open court shown at the beginning of the play. It could be argued that this is one way in which the play enacts a sense of change between Lear's kingdom and that of his daughters.

Such minor characters may seem to have no importance in and of themselves. This can be very much the case when one simply reads the plays as pieces of literature. But their inclusion points to another dimension: the performance. These parts exist in order to resonate with the broader interests of the play as a whole, and this is something worth noting in assessments.

Tutorial

Study tips

1 When dealing with major characters, keep a note of when those characters appear on stage. Work out how often they speak, and to whom. If you find out that an important figure shifts attention between several other characters at any point, then you need to think about how the main character can be played. This is a different situation from one in which a single protagonist does most of the speaking. What are the implications for the presentation of the main figures?

2 Especially in the histories, a profusion of less important characters can become overwhelming. These figures may have been familiar to Shakespeare's contemporaries, but they seem difficult to portray effectively to a modern audience. Try to keep track of which characters appear in which scenes, and work out how they could be performed in order to give them some importance.

Discussion points

1 How do you make a stock role work for a modern audience? Are there examples that you feel are simply too much part of Renaissance culture to translate well into a more modern sensibility?

2 Even if a major protagonist has elements of stock characterisation, does the role nevertheless contain more modern elements of identity and individuality?

3 The play you are studying may require a great deal of interaction between important characters. How does the play help the audience focus on this interaction?

4 Some of the plays, especially the histories, seem to delegate women to the sidelines. Is this something that marks the plays as being of their period? Is it something you would want to change? Would you want to draw attention to the issue if you were directing a performance?

Practical assignments

1 Divide the characters of a play you are studying into major protagonists on the one hand and less important figures on the other. How many of each type have elements of stock characterisation about them? If this includes the main roles, what does it say about Renaissance dramatic conventions? Does it imply that a contemporary audience would be looking for something different from what a modern audience would take for granted?

2 Watch two film or video versions of a play. Look out for scenes from the text that are cut in performance. Why does the director choose to remove them? Why would Shakespeare have included them in the first place, and what makes them seem irrelevant to people from a later period?

Practice questions

1 How do two Shakespeare plays compare in terms of their focus on the main protagonists?

2 Are women presented differently from men when they fulfil the role of a major protagonist?

3 To what extent does a play depend on major roles, as opposed to ensemble group acting?

5 Analysing the Text

One-minute overview

Shakespeare's plays contain language that is almost proverbially rich. He lived at a time when the English language was changing radically and his plays draw from a great range of vocabulary as a result. You will find elements from the classical languages and from contemporary Europe in addition to English itself. This chapter will introduce you to the techniques Shakespeare adopted when constructing the lines and speeches that make up the spoken elements of the plays.

The chapter has been divided into:
- Iambic verse
- Rhyme patterns
- Blank verse
- Feminine endings
- Other verse forms
- Prose
- Set pieces
- Interaction

Iambic Verse

The writing of verse is a structured activity. It is naive to imagine the poet sitting in a garret beside a guttering candle, composing great works of inspiration. The various English poetic forms have rules, which are derived from other languages, including Greek and Latin. An epic poem such as Virgil's *Aeneid* is written in a different metre from a short poem by Catullus. Perhaps the most common form is the iambic pentameter, so called because it divides the line into five 'feet' or sections, each of which consists of an iambic pattern. The iamb has one short syllable followed by one long, so that the line looks like the first line of Shakespeare's Sonnet 12:

∨ - ∨ - ∨ - ∨ - ∨ -

When I do count the clock that tells the time

This is a very good example of a regular line, one that fits the pattern of stresses. Not all lines are, however, perfectly regular.

Rhyme Patterns

Additionally, the specific type of poetry will have a rhyme pattern. Shakespeare's sonnets use a structure of three sets of four lines (quatrains) followed by a concluding couplet. Each quatrain has alternating rhymes, so that the rhyme structure of one of his sonnets is usually:

1st Quatrain: (abab)
2nd Quatrain: (cdcd)
3rd Quatrain: (efef)
Couplet: (gg)

So, to continue with Sonnet 12, the first quatrain looks like this:

- When I do count the clock that tells the time,
- And see the brave day sunk in hideous night;
- When I behold the violet past prime,
- And sable curls all silver'd o'er with white,

The rhyme is time-night-prime-white, or (abab). In the second and third quatrains the pattern is identical, but the sounds change. The final two lines round it all off with their own rhyme. This is almost mathematical in its precision. Sometimes a specific rhyme pattern is introduced. The effect draws the audience's attention towards the unexpected repetition. This happens most commonly at the end of a scene, when change is about to happen. It rounds things off and prepares for new movement:

Cheerly to sea! The signs of war advance!
No king of England, if not king of France! (*Henry V* II.ii.192–193)

Overall, the effect provides a closure similar to the concluding couplet in a sonnet; even modern audiences, both in the theatre and watching a film, are able to notice such an obvious addition to the poetry.

Blank Verse

The importance of metre and rhyme lies not so much in which schemes are used as in how they are manipulated, and how they are related to one another. This is because when Shakespeare writes sections of the plays in poetic form, he uses blank verse. It is iambic in form, but without any rhyme scheme.

The rules of English poetry use classical terminology, but there is one crucial difference: Latin and Greek verse is based on syllable length; English poetry is based on stress (another technical term for this is 'accent', and this does not refer to the part of the world you come from). The poetic rhythms in Shakespeare take advantage of the peculiarities of English verse.

The standard iambic line sounds odd. Regularity in spoken language is noticeable because it sounds unnatural. Read out the first line of sonnet 12 again: it deliberately echoes the sound pattern of a clock, both in its monotonous beat and in its uses of alliteration, or sound patterns, on the letters *c* and *t*. But in drama, variety of expression is a necessity. So Shakespeare often departs from the rules of iambic verse in order to lay even more stress on an element of the line:

∨ - ∨ - ∨ - ∨ - ∨   -
To be, or not to be, that is the question (*Hamlet* III.i.55)

You will notice that according to the strict interpretation of the stress pattern, the word 'that' is unstressed, but when the line is spoken it is much more logical and sensible to place stress on the word. It is this common-sense realisation that standard English is different from poetic patterns that is the key to the whole issue of Shakespeare's use of blank verse. So it is only partly true to say that his poetry is structured according to the iambic pentameter; it is more precisely correct to say that what really matters is how this structure plays off against normal spoken English. A line that goes against the grain of the metre can have at least a subliminal effect. The result is an unusual emphasis that is linked to rhetorical effects.

Feminine Endings

A peculiarity produced by the relationship we have been discussing is the so-called 'feminine' line ending. It occurs when the line ends in a downbeat or unstressed syllable, in addition to the standard iambic pattern. The famous line from *Hamlet* quoted above is a good example. In fact the first eight lines of this speech all have feminine endings. One of the most famous speeches in English is therefore irregular.

Other Verse Forms

Sometimes a playwright will use metrical forms that are different from blank verse. One of the most well known comes with the witches in *Macbeth*:

- When shall we three meet again?
- In thunder, lightning, or in rain? (I.i.1–2)

They are always using verse patterns and rhymes in a way that obviously differentiates them from the rest of the action. The shorter lines couple with the rhyming to give their utterances something of the character of a chant. The technique underscores their riddling nature and so affects the action of the play in a very specific manner.

Prose

Shakespeare's plays also use the ordinary spoken word. Usually this is done to mark off an individual or small group as different from others. A play might have some nobles indulging in flights of poetic fancy while the servants speak normally. The effect is to heighten the differences between the two groups and this is commonly accomplished in relation to social status. An example can be found in *Romeo and Juliet*, when the audience is given some idea of the preparations for the Capulet masque (I.v) and again for Juliet's impending wedding to Paris (IV.iv).

Such scenes not only show another dimension to the play world but can also act as a commentary on the pretensions and anxieties of the masters. Perhaps the most famous examples are the gravediggers in *Hamlet* (V.i) and the porter in *Macbeth* (II.iii).

Prose can also be used by more exalted figures, sometimes to denote private conversation. The plotting between Goneril and Regan in *King Lear* begins immediately after they have been invested with power. This long scene sees the old King dividing the kingdom and spurning Cordelia. She speaks with her sisters before leaving with her new husband, the King of France. Finally the two remaining sisters discuss in prose how best to proceed in relation to their father (I.i.283ff). The use of prose in a private conversation inevitably places it in juxtaposition with the preceding events.

Set Pieces

Many schools still require their pupils to learn chunks of Shakespeare by heart. Fortunately, this is not something you will be doing. However, the tendency does point to an important issue. How does a long, set-piece speech work as part of its play? In *Julius Caesar*, Brutus speaks to the people of Rome after the death of Caesar in prose, which is most unusual (III.ii.12ff). It is then followed by Antony's famous oration (III.ii.73ff). The narrative patterning of the two speeches is heightened by means of comparisons between them. The understated prose of Brutus is completely undone by the poetic power of what comes after.

Some plays contain noticeably more of these speeches than others, one example being *Henry V*. The association between the heroic figure of the King and the long poetic speech considerably strengthens his powerful status in the play. A similar effect can be seen in *Richard III*, especially at the outset. Here the plotting figure of the Duke of Gloucester seems unstoppable, and the power of his language reinforces the point. *The Tempest* similarly provides Prospero with another series of set speeches.

Shakespeare used all of the resources available to him when composing such a speech. One trick to watch out for is the line or group of lines composed mainly or completely of monosyllables. When Othello is listening to Iago's manipulations (*Othello* III.iii) his responses are composed almost entirely of words of one syllable:

- Dost thou say so? (205)
- And so she did. (207)
- I am bound to thee for ever. (213)

The effect is to emphasise that Othello is mulling over what Iago tells him, reducing his responses to practically nothing. The actor is given a choice here in terms of the speed of the interaction with Iago. At what pace should these short words be spoken? Are they hurried, to reinforce the speed at which Iago succeeds in making Othello jealous of Desdemona? Or are they more measured, to bring out the full force of the change? Such lines are good examples of the limitations of study that pays attention only to the written text as you have it before you.

Interaction

There are several elements of the text of a play that are not easily apparent on a first reading. Some cannot be ascertained from reading at all. The whole array of possible character interactions is crucial in performance, but the written play you will be studying is not a reliable guide as to how these are carried out.

The easiest way to come to terms with the problem is by means of spacing. Not physical space on the stage – this is something to which we will be returning in Chapter 6. The space between lines or speeches also contributes to interaction. For example, a play may contain several of the long set speeches we have just been discussing. How do the other characters react to it?

Sometimes this can be determined by who speaks next. Is it someone who is friendly with the previous speaker? Is it someone hostile? How long should the gap be between speech and response? Sometimes the speech is designed to be followed by action, as in King Henry's oration at Harfleur (*Henry V* III.i) exhorting his troops to exploit a breach made in the walls. Other speeches are in soliloquy form, for example in *Hamlet* or *Richard III*. In such cases the delivery of the speech is aimed entirely at the audience, and interaction with other characters is irrelevant.

Shakespeare varies the ways in which characters respond to one another. He even goes so far as to break up a single line, sometimes several times. This technique works with the metrical pattern to produce a combination of flowing language:

Camillo:	I am appointed by him to murther you.
Polixenes:	By whom, Camillo?
Camillo:	By the King.
Polixenes:	For what?
	(*The Winter's Tale* I.ii.412–413)

The second line of the two given here is broken up into three sections. This division of the poetry tends to speed up the interaction, giving it an urgent intensity. You will need to be aware of just how character interaction is informed by such verbal movements.

Tutorial

Study tips

1 Look at the shape of the words on the page of a play. Is the scene broken up into small sections? Is it composed of large set pieces? Is there subtle movement between various characters as they share a large section of poetry? Does a block of prose stand out? The answers to these questions

should point you to various techniques of language expression that are being exploited by the playwright.

2 When studying a play, work out which of the various forms of language and verse tend to be associated with which characters. Does one tend to use longer set pieces of poetry than others, or are there variations? This kind of analysis can tell you a great deal about the ways in which language reinforces character interaction.

Discussion points

1 When a play shifts from one major mode to another, what does this signify, both in terms of plot development and character interaction?

2 How should variations in rhyme and metre be linked to the overall performance? Characterisation is important here. If a major figure tends to use the same range of techniques, what does this say about him or her?

Practical assignments

1 Go to a library and borrow at least one sound recording of a play you are studying. Because of the medium, you will find yourself concentrating on how the speech and verse patterns influence your understanding of the language of a play.

2 Turn off the sound while watching a video performance of a major section of the text. Watch how the actors relate with one another in terms of physical use of space. Then watch the same sequence again with the sound turned on. Does the full performance reinforce your prior analysis, or does it do something unexpected?

3 If you are intending to use a specific section of text in an assessment, spend some time delineating the stress pattern. If, when you speak the lines out loud, they seem naturally to vary from the standard metrical pattern you are expecting, what does this say about the lines themselves? Is it likely that the emphasis has been shifted to draw attention to a particular word or phrase? This exercise is a practical method of coming to grips with verse, and helps focus your attention on how it is integrated into the play.

Practice questions

1 Compare the use of set-piece speeches in your chosen plays.

2 Discuss how a play's language changes according to differences between the various groups who speak.

3 How is character interaction affected by the kinds of language employed?

6 Performing the Plays

One-minute overview

Shakespeare's plays were constructed for a very different set of performance and cultural circumstances from those of today. The logic of their composition and performance was therefore designed for a specific set of requirements. These are radically different from the requirements not only of modern film and video media, but of the modern stage as well.

This chapter will discuss:
■ Itinerant players
■ The London theatres: culture
■ The London theatres: location
■ The London theatres: architecture
■ Audience composition
■ Zonal staging
■ Choreography
■ Emblematic acting
■ Modern performance

Itinerant Players

By the late Middle Ages, enough talent and wealth had been generated for travelling troupes of players to be formed. These would go from town to town according to the feast and market days and would perform a medley of plays. As with other travellers, they would stay at the many inns that dotted the trade and communications routes. They would do deals with the owners of the inns, putting on short plays for profit and splitting the proceeds. The innkeepers would supply the premises and the players would entertain the guests. A makeshift stage would be set up in the inn courtyards and people would pay depending on the quality of the view and comfort.

Two crucial developments had by now occurred: people were prepared to pay for entertainment in dramatic form and the players themselves had developed a whole series of performance techniques based on the circumstances in which they performed.

The London Theatres: Culture

It was only a matter of time before the next logical development took place. The burgeoning growth of the metropolis of London gave many a chance to get rich quick, and the new theatre professionals were no exception. Groups of theatre entrepreneurs began to emerge and, in 1576, both the Theatre and the Blackfriars were opened. The Red Lion had been in existence since 1565, but the explosive growth in the playhouses, marked by the new buildings that sprung up from the 1570s on, makes it clear that London had entered upon a new era in popular entertainment.

The prior religious associations of the drama were now suspect in an age of religious conflict. We know that Shakespeare himself had been to see religious plays as a boy in central England. The new players were technically vagabonds, since they owed allegiance to no master. This period provides many examples of a society in rapid flux. Conceptions of social order based on the old feudal system of land ownership were fast becoming out of date. The players were new men of a kind rarely seen before and, in common with many others, they made their way by means of money and business, not in relation to a class system based on landed wealth. Many economic historians label this time as 'mercantilist'.

All of this goes some way towards explaining why theatrical troupes sought aristocratic and even royal patronage. It also explains why Shakespeare felt it necessary not only to pay off his family's debts but also to buy a coat of arms and become a landowner himself. His rank was thereby raised to that of the gentry. Incidentally, this is another example of the kind of language change we have already encountered. The modern meaning of 'gentle' is far removed from the social meanings of the term in the Renaissance.

The imprecise and somewhat dubious nature of the theatrical profession caused other problems. Issues of religion loomed large and had critical effects on political and social processes. The conflicts engendered were complex. Although the Anglican Church was the established religion, many of its services were still very close in form to those of the Catholic Church, while at the same time its doctrines were Calvinist. There were differences of opinion between different kinds of Protestant.

The London Theatres: Location

Since the Reformation, the City of London had tended towards the more extreme forms of Protestantism. This was to make life difficult for the players, since the City authorities regarded them at best as a dangerous nuisance. The theatres were considered by some to be hotbeds of sedition; they were certainly immoral. Given this climate, the strategy the players adopted was to build their theatres in carefully chosen locations.

The most obvious of these was Southwark. This area, on the south side of the Thames, was a suburb and so was technically outside the jurisdiction of the City of London, except in times of emergency. It was still close enough that people could get to it quite easily, since all they had to do was cross London Bridge. It should therefore come as no surprise to find that this is indeed where many of the theatres were erected. Southwark became something of an entertainment centre. Bear-baiting pits, bull-baiting pits, cock-fighting dens, gambling houses, taverns, brothels and playhouses all mingled together in very close proximity.

Additionally, certain areas within the walls of the City were designated as 'Liberties', with similar exemptions to the suburbs. Perhaps the most famous of these was the Blackfriars, which housed a serious rival to the suburban theatres. It was subsequently taken over by Shakespeare's company. The Blackfriars theatre was unusual in that it was indoors. It therefore needed illumination and was more expensive than the outdoor theatres such as the Globe.

Shakespeare's later plays all take advantage of the possibilities for complex action afforded by a more elaborate and more expensive staging capacity.

The London Theatres: Architecture

When the outdoor theatres were constructed, the pattern followed was a familiar one. The amphitheatre shape was adopted, and indeed the bear-baiting pit in Southwark that pre-dated the theatres also used this design. The theatres were broadly circular, although the actual construction was probably multi-sided – for example, 12 or 20 sides give the overall impression of a circular building.

Internally the buildings were shaped in accordance with the tradition of playacting we have already discussed. The stage was set against one wall, but it did not take up the whole length of the wall. It also jutted out into the middle of the audience. The back wall of the stage was the tiring-house, where all of the company's materials were kept, including props, costumes and items unique to that particular group. Here is a plan of such a building:

**Fig. 4:
Plan of open-air
theatre**

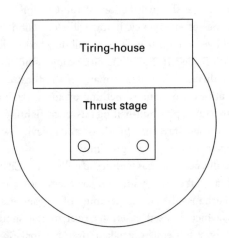

This stage has two pillars to support its roof. At the rear of the stage would have been two doors leading directly into the tiring-house. There would also be a raised dais set against the back wall, behind which some of the stages would have had an alcove that could be used for various parts of the play. There would also be a balcony so that the facing wall of the tiring-house could be fully utilised in all three dimensions (remember the balcony scene in *Romeo and Juliet*?). There may also have been stairs leading down into the audience; these were probably portable.

The audience surrounded the stage on at least three sides. The 'groundlings' were nearest the stage and were on the ground floor, as the nickname suggests. They were in the part of the theatre that would later evolve into the orchestra pit, and they were at the mercy of the elements. They paid a penny each for the privilege. Wealthier patrons, however, could pay for a place in the galleries that ran around the inside walls, and which were covered. The higher you went, the more you paid. Some people paid to have seats on the stage itself, or even behind the stage on the tiring-house balcony.

Audience Composition

Given the massive disparity in cost between different parts of the audience, there was also a corresponding disparity in social composition. The groundlings were notoriously rowdy. Many of them were apprentices out for some entertainment after a hard week's work. But also, in the most expensive locations, there would be lords and ladies of the realm. Combined with the fractured perspectives possible in such a building, it may be misleading to think of this as a single audience at all. It is certainly radically different from the usual theatre audience we think of now, sitting quietly in a dark auditorium and all seeing the play from more or less the same angle. The modern stage is detached from its audience in a way that would be foreign to a Renaissance theatregoer. This is a direct result of the shape of the stage itself. The modern stage is set wholly against one wall, divided from its viewers. But Shakespeare's stage was thrust out into the middle of some of the noisiest people in London. How would the cast deal with such a situation? How would a playwright cope with the varied expectations of different parts of the audience?

Zonal Staging

The Renaissance audience was like a crowd of spectators at a football match. Not only were they diverse in their interests, but they could also see one another, as well as the actors. If a play does not go well in these circumstances, it soon becomes obvious. One part of the audience will affect another, until the performance is drowned out. If one part of the audience is disaffected it soon spreads, like a Mexican wave effect in a sports stadium.

There are, however, ways to focus this audience's interests. A playwright in this period had to keep his audience engaged. That meant conducting a balancing act between complex plotting and sophisticated intrigue for those who wanted them, and straightforward action for those who didn't. The culture of performance that developed was supremely successful at managing its audience. This necessity goes a long way to explaining the richness associated with the drama of Shakespeare and his contemporaries.

One the biggest advantages the acting company had was the stage itself. Unlike the modern shape, the thrust stage allows a greater variation in the amount and types of space available to the actors. It is much deeper, so layered effects are more believable in performance. Different parts of the stage can become associated in the audience's minds with different kinds of action, or even specific characters. Shakespeare's plays make great use of such symbolic associations. The front edges of the stage are situated right out in the middle of the audience, a prime location for direct audience-actor interaction. In contrast, the area towards the rear of the stage is as far from the audience as the actors can go, marking it as less intimate and more formal. These different areas of the stage are called zones, and the best way to describe how they work is to take a specific example. We will be discussing the start of *Hamlet*. The beginning of any play is crucial in the way that it introduces the action, and this exercise will give you an idea of how the play might have been enacted on its own stage.

The example of *Hamlet*

The best way to proceed is to place yourself in the role of director. How do you want the characters to move and interact? Which parts of the stage do you want them to utilise? The play opens with two sentries meeting while on night watch:

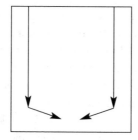

◄
**Fig. 5.1:
The sentries
meet**

The diagram above suggests that they enter from different doors, patrol the edges of the stage, and then meet at the very front of the stage, right in the middle of the audience. Here they speak the first 13 lines of the play. Then Horatio and Marcellus enter, approach the guards and greet them. One of the sentinels, Francisco, leaves having finished his watch. The remaining soldier, Barnardo, begins to discuss with the others what he has seen on his watch.

So far, this seems straightforward enough. However, it accomplishes a great deal more than just starting off a play. First of all, it establishes an intimacy between these characters and the audience, partly because of the zone of the stage on which the scene is played out and partly because the sentinels are of roughly equivalent social status to the groundlings in the audience. In effect, they are in very close physical proximity to characters to which they can relate. Secondly, the fact that something is very wrong is quickly made apparent to the audience.

But Shakespeare now introduces a change of pace. Rather than have Barnardo continue to relate what he has seen, he interrupts the group by showing the King's ghost on stage:

**Fig. 5.2:
The group sees
the ghost**

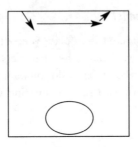

Here the group of actors observes the ghost pass silently across the rear of stage, moving from one door to the other. A visual distance is opened up between the zone at the front edge of the stage and that at the rear. The audience, in complicity with the three characters, watches the ghost at a distance. The play immediately sets up a crucial symbolic differentiation between the zones, one that will become a major axis of meaning for the action as a whole. The front of the stage will be associated with characters with whom the audience can identify, or at least sympathise. The rear is for action, characters and events that are distanced from the audience. This performance aspect of the play reinforces the action.

Choreography

The ways in which the characters interact or are distanced from one another can greatly affect how the audience perceives them and relates to them. The way in which this is managed on such a stage is similar to dance choreography. For our purposes the kind of choreography envisaged is one that relates to the zones of the stage, and this of course changes from play to play.

We have already looked briefly at a section of *Hamlet*, but other plays provide much more complex instances of movement in action. *A Midsummer Night's Dream* contains a scene in which the four lovers are all asleep on different parts of the stage (IV.i). At the same time, Bottom is asleep with

Titania. Oberon and Puck come on, wake up Titania, then leave with her, all reconciled. Then Theseus, Hippolyta and the rest of the court of Athens arrive, wake up the lovers, are reconciled with them and then all leave together. Finally, Bottom wakes up and recounts his dream. Here the audience is being asked to believe that six people are all asleep on the same stage, but separated, and to watch the awakenings taking place one by one. This is zonal staging taken to its logical extreme.

There are also many instances of characters manipulating one another, for example the play within a play motif, such as the 'Mousetrap' in *Hamlet* (III.ii). The play as a whole is full of people carefully watching or spying on one another, and the mousetrap foregrounds the problem. Hamlet must use the space of the stage to be able to watch the effect of the play upon Claudius while, at the same time, commenting upon it directly to the audience.

Choreography on this stage must therefore include the audience as a partner. The level of interaction between cast and audience that is made possible by the shape of the stage requires the audience to be managed in just as sophisticated a manner as the actors. Indeed, for these purposes, the audience is another actor. At a basic level, this is often denoted in modern editions by the use of 'asides' as stage directions. But this does not simply mean that Hamlet, for example, is throwing comments over his shoulder at the audience. Rather, it shows points at which the character is in direct communication with the audience.

Following on from our earlier discussion of the zones of the stage, it is now possible for us to imagine just how close the interaction between actor and audience was at the front of the stage. But of course this relationship does not remain stable; Hamlet goes upstage to talk with the ghost, breaking his rapport with the audience. It is possible for a cunning playwright to use the downstage zone of audience identification as a way of manipulating his audience's responses. This is what happens with the Machiavel figures such as Richard III, or Edmund in *King Lear*. By speaking a soliloquy directly to the audience, they embroil the audience in prior knowledge of their plans. A form of dramatic irony results, in which the audience knows more than many of the characters. Iago in *Othello* is the greatest practitioner of this technique, playing with the audience just as he plays with Othello himself. Instead of the downstage zone being occupied by a sympathetic character, it is under the control of an arch-manipulator, and there is nothing the audience can do about it. This, of course, reinforces Iago's powers of persuasion.

Emblematic Acting

The acting techniques required for the Renaissance stage are entirely different from those so familiar to us. On this stage, the actors need to be open to many kinds of movement and interaction that go well beyond the bounds of possibility on a closed modern stage. They also need to deal with a potentially disruptive audience, one that almost entirely surrounds them. It is not enough simply to perform movements and deliver speeches to a relatively fixed, single point, as it is with most modern theatres. How can an actor combine all of these requirements in an effective and coherent manner?

The single most important observation to be made here seems revolutionary, but is in fact startlingly simple. Most modern acting techniques fail on such a stage. Characters have to be portrayed in a way that makes them accessible to different parts of a contradictory audience simultaneously. There is no fixed point, therefore mobility is an absolute must. The actors must be outgoing, versatile and willing to engage at a moment's notice with a different part of the audience. This is exactly the opposite of what is required of a modern performer, who can focus on one point of attention, whether it be a camera or a theatre audience. Modern techniques of psychological coherence would be of dubious value in the Renaissance stage environment, which relates to comments made about character psychology in Chapter 4.

In such a potentially noisy atmosphere, intense characterisation would be lost. The style of acting needed is known as 'emblematic', or 'gestural', since it requires a special kind of unity between word, gesture and movement. Characters are to be portrayed on this stage, not enacted from the inside. It is no coincidence that many Renaissance plays are aware of the kind of acting required. They seem to revel in their sheer artificiality, drawing attention to the fact that they are plays. In *Hamlet*, Polonius talks about his own abilities as an actor when he played the part of Julius Caesar (III.ii.103), and critics have long maintained that the original actor playing Polonius in *Hamlet* did play Caesar in Shakespeare's slightly earlier play. This is only one of many possible examples of a self-referentiality that denies our modern sense of realism.

The use of props reinforces the emblematic techniques. In *Othello*, for example, there is the famous problem of the handkerchief. Othello blows it out of all proportion and comes to see it as damning evidence of his wife's adultery. Many modern commentators have problems with this, because in terms of modern character psychology it simply makes no sense. But one may turn the problem on its head: in relation to Renaissance acting, modern character psychology makes no sense. The handkerchief draws the audience's attention to an easily identifiable piece of stage property. Othello's relationship with it acts as an emblem of his obsessions; in terms of the play's immediate cultural context, the importance of the handkerchief makes perfect sense. The enactment of a role is what matters, not how internally consistent that role might be.

Modern Performance

Most courses that contain a Shakespeare element work almost entirely from the text. At best, there might be a screening of a film or video version of a play, or the possibility of one or two trips to the theatre. More advanced or focused courses might build these elements into the curriculum. But you will have to remember that no modern performance will fully be able to recreate a Shakespeare play exactly as it would have been performed in the Renaissance. The closest is perhaps the reconstructed Globe Theatre in London, although even that has had problems with its performances. This is due to the fact that modern audiences are not used to the massively different culture of a performance in the Renaissance style.

Since all modern performances are necessarily versions, you will have to look out for ways in which they are flavoured by the predilections of the director and cast. In a sense, there are no modern versions that are fully efficient representations of Shakespeare's plays. This is not only because of the vast gap between the cultures, but also an inevitable outcome of the fact that film, video or modern stage productions are different media from the stage of Shakespeare's time.

This means that a modern production is always caught in a dilemma: how true does one try to remain to the text? If one plays it as 'straight' as possible, the play will be boring or even incomprehensible to a modern audience. Some modern productions, such as Trevor Nunn's famous Royal Shakespeare Company *Macbeth* with Judi Dench and Ian McKellen, attempt to be as minimalist as possible. The video version is commercially available (produced in 1978) and is directly based on the stage production. But even here sound and lighting effects are available in a way unknown to Shakespeare.

From your point of view, what matters most is how useful a particular production is for the purposes of study. Perhaps you need a performance that tries to stay as close as possible to the spirit of the original. The BBC Shakespeare series is a well-known attempt to do just this. Unfortunately it can seem dated now, and certainly most of the plays in the series are not at all innovative. This can sometimes get in the way of how useful a performance might be to you.

Alternatively, you may wish to experiment with versions of the plays that try to be unusually effective. Joseph Mankiewicz's 1953 film of *Julius Caesar* uses the techniques of expressionism to enhance the importance of the storm before Caesar's death. After Cassius' Machiavel speech at the end of I.ii, Mankiewicz shows the storm beginning in the forum itself and then shifts to the next few scenes of conspiratorial darkness. The director has used the new techniques available to him through the medium of film to enhance the meaning of the play.

A modern production is in itself a sort of critical commentary. This will tell you a great deal not only about the play but also about the context of the film itself. The films of Laurence Olivier are a case in point. *Henry V* was filmed just before the Normandy landings in 1944, although it was not released until afterwards. Olivier conflates scenes by removing sections that demonstrate the vicious side of Henry's war against France. This applies to most of III.iii, in which the horrors of war are described as they are about to be visited upon Harfleur. Olivier's film is a piece of brilliant propaganda for the Allied war effort in 1944, so Henry must be shown as a kind of liberator.

Similarly, in his film of *Hamlet,* Olivier uses voiceover for the 'To be, or not to be' soliloquy (III.i.55ff). This internalises the monologue, enhancing the purely psychological interpretation of Prince Hamlet as a fully realised modern individual. You could argue, therefore, that this violates Shakespeare's text in order to produce a specific interpretation.

Ultimately, what matters is how much the performance material helps you with your course. You may not have the time to devote to seeing performances, and you may feel that the Shakespeare component of your course does not merit the extra effort required. However, these were plays, not the literature they have subsequently become, and you will be missing an opportunity to gain further insight (and, probably, a higher assessment grade) if you ignore performance entirely.

Tutorial

Study tips

1 When you are studying a scene, try to envisage how the characters would interact on the stage. Put yourself in the actors' shoes.

2 It is very difficult to keep track of the many minor roles that exist in some plays, especially the histories. When you are dealing with such a play, imagine a face for each character, perhaps from your own life experience. For example, if a play contains many minor nobles who end up being executed, give bit parts in your mind to former schoolfriends, teachers, shopkeepers, people you like or people you dislike – anything that will help you make sense of quick shifts in the play.

Discussion points

1 How does the standard shape of the modern stage change the ways in which a Renaissance play is performed now?

2 What new techniques are available to a film production that would not have been around in Shakespeare's own times? How could these be used to advantage? Are there any that, in your opinion, would detract from a film version and which you would rather not use?

Practical assignments

1 Watch at least two film or video versions of a play, such as Olivier's and Branagh's *Henry V*. In what ways do they differ? In what ways are they similar? How do they compare as interpretations?

2 If you go to a production of a play in the theatre, take note of the use of space, movement and props. Analyse for yourself the ways in which a modern stage production interprets the play.

3 Draw up two lists of how you would direct a stage version of a play you are studying. The first has an unlimited budget and can be as sumptuous as you wish. The second is to be minimalist and the use of elements such as costuming and props and has to be symbolic. How do these compare?

Practice questions

1 How does a performance with which you are familiar interpret the play to suit its own ends?

2 How might a modern film or stage production challenge the perceptions and assumptions of a modern audience in a way that seems fresh?

3 How might the play you are studying have been performed on the Renaissance stage?

One-minute overview

This chapter will point you towards contextual information on the history, politics, society and culture of the English Renaissance. It is impossible to detail every possible aspect of the period that impinged on Shakespeare's plays, so the chapter is divided into sections introducing some of the major issues. Each section has some suggestions for further reading on that topic.

There will be material on:
- Social status
- The monarchy
- The economy
- Religion
- Gender
- Europe and beyond

Social Status

The Renaissance English were obsessed with status. They defined themselves in relation to their place in the social hierarchy and, by extension, in terms of how they related to others. They did not see their individual identity as the prime marker of their sense of selfhood and in this they differed markedly from their modern descendants. This is not to say that they did not pursue their own interests, but it does imply that they had a very clear sense of what was possible for them to achieve in the limited social mobility available to them.

Even so, massive social changes were taking place throughout the period. The drive towards the accumulation of monetary wealth as the basis of prestige had already begun, and was to become increasingly associated with the rise of the

British Empire. However, society still defined itself in terms of the old feudal conception of land ownership. The monarch stood at the apex of a complex social pyramid, which widened ever downward in a sophisticated series of minor social gradations.

Needless to say, the old conception of the social order was very often at variance with hard economic fact. London merchants could be wealthier than some of the high nobility, and there was a great deal of nervousness about how to reinforce a proper sense of rank. Elizabeth's reign in particular saw a massive rise in the amount of sumptuary legislation. This is the technical term for laws that governed the amounts and relative values of clothing and other personal displays that were permitted to each rank. All of this betrays an awareness of the fact that outward appearance did not necessarily accord with one's position in society.

The best way to unravel the social complexities of this culture is to read about it. It is extremely useful to target aspects of the plays you are studying by means of carefully chosen secondary reading. Choose books that deal directly with the areas you have identified for study. Here are some examples:

- Lisa Jardine, *Reading Shakespeare Historically* (London: Routledge, 1996)
- D.M Palliser, *The Age of Elizabeth: England Under the Later Tudors 1547–1603* (Essex: Longman, 1992)
- Lawrence Stone, *The Crisis of the Aristocracy 1558–1641* (Abridged Edition; London: Oxford University Press, 1967)

The Monarchy

The history of the Tudor dynasty is full of instances of extreme paranoia about their right to the throne, and about possible challenges to it. This anxiety was well founded, since they themselves were usurpers with a very tenuous claim to the crown. Here is a list of the reigns of the English monarchs from the time of Edward III:

Edward III	:	1327–1377
Richard II	:	1377–1399
Henry IV	:	1399–1413
Henry V	:	1413–1422
Henry VI	:	1422–1461
Edward IV	:	1461–1483
Richard III	:	1483–1485
Henry VII	:	1485–1509
Henry VIII	:	1509–1547
Edward VI	:	1547–1553
Mary I	:	1553–1558
Elizabeth I	:	1558–1603
James I	:	1603–1625

◀
Fig. 6:
Chronological table of the English monarchy

Henry Tudor came to the throne as a result of the defeat and death of Richard III at the Battle of Bosworth. Henry was the last claimant associated with the House of Lancaster and, by marrying the heiress Elizabeth of York, he ended the Wars of the Roses.

However, Henry was still plagued by rival claimants, mainly because his own claim was dubious to say the least. It was based on his descent from John of Gaunt, one of Edward III's younger sons, through Henry's mother, Margaret Beaufort. The problem with this lineage was that the Beauforts were the offspring of John of Gaunt's love affair with Katherine Swynford. This adulterous liaison was legitimised by the issuing of a papal bull at the instigation of Richard II, who needed his powerful uncle's support at the time, but the whole affair was tainted by scandal. So the claim of Henry Tudor to the English throne was not only based on inheritance through a woman, but was traced back to a line that was originally illegitimate.

Even so, Henry VII managed to hold on to the throne, mainly because he was an extremely astute politician. He was able to keep most of the upper echelons of the nobility happy and, together with memories of the bloodletting of the Wars of the Roses, they generally supported the new dynasty. Henry was also helped by the fecundity of his marriage, which produced an heir – Prince Arthur – and a spare – Prince Henry.

Arthur died young and young Henry came to the throne in a blaze of magnificence. However, his marital career was not a conspicuous success, with well-known results. It led to the dissolution of the link with the Church of Rome, an event of momentous historical significance. He was succeeded in turn by each of his three children (all by different wives). Stability was not restored until the reign of Elizabeth I, who had herself been declared illegitimate by her own father.

Elizabeth learned a hard lesson from the events of her childhood and early adulthood. She played the game of marriage diplomacy with great skill. England was in a powerful strategic position, just on the flank of the contest for continental supremacy between France and Spain. Elizabeth was able (mostly) to keep England out of the conflict and also to remain unmarried. It is from this period that we begin to see the emergence of the underlying principle of British foreign policy, the balance of power, in which Britain played one side off against the other, always ensuring that no single European state predominated on the continent. And, of course, in the meantime the British Empire grew and grew. Elizabeth was succeeded by her relative James VI of Scotland, who finally united the crowns of mainland Britain as James I of England.

All of this necessarily impinges on Shakespeare's work. We have already seen how anxieties about state power permeate the plays, and they relate to the history of their own time in ways that we are only beginning to unravel. Here are some suggestions for further reading:

- Lisa Hopkins, *Women Who Would Be Kings: Female Rulers of the Seventeenth Century* (London: Vision Press, 1991)
- Carole Levin, *The Heart and Stomach of a King: Elizabeth I and the Politics of Sex and Power* (Philadelphia: University of Pennsylvania Press, 1994)
- Alison Weir, *Elizabeth the Queen* (London: Pimlico, 1999)

The Economy

As well as being the basis for social prestige, land ownership was still the main driving force behind the economy.

Management of the land was a priority and, when the country suffered from agricultural problems, there were widespread social effects. For example, a series of bad harvests during the reign of Queen Mary increased social tensions, heightening resentment of her religious policies. There were similar problems again in the 1590s.

Of course, England was a major trading nation. The country's geographical position encouraged overseas trade in a way that set the foundations for the British Empire. Trade was therefore closely connected with politics. The concerns of the cloth merchants, for example, greatly influenced Elizabeth's balancing act in relation to the revolts against Spanish rule in the Netherlands. The growth of England as a seafaring power was a necessary defence against Spanish aggression in particular, and the spectacular defeat of the great Spanish Armada in 1588 cemented the reputation of England's navy. The economy was badly affected by ongoing wars, of course, but then the opportunities for plundering Spanish treasure ships were plentiful, and the Queen did very nicely when she helped fund the attacks.

Rising inflation was a serious problem, not only in England but also throughout Western Europe. One of the main reasons for this was the influx of extra coinage as a result of Spanish exploitation of the mines of South America. The opening up of the Americas was beginning to be very lucrative, and of course Britain's long-term role was of major historical importance. The most accessible and informative analysis of European economics and culture of the period is:

- Fernand Braudel, *Civilization and Capitalism, 15th–18th Century* (3 vols; London: Fontana Press, 1985)

Religion

When Henry VIII decided to divorce his wife, Catherine of Aragon, he unleashed forces that have had a profound effect on the development of the British Isles. Catherine had previously been married to Henry's elder brother, Prince

Arthur, who had died at the age of 16. She married Henry when he became king, although they had to be granted a papal dispensation in order for the marriage to take place. This was because they were within the forbidden degrees of affinity, since Catherine was Henry's sister-in-law.

When it later became clear that Catherine could not provide Henry with the male heir he so desperately needed to ensure the continuation of the Tudor dynasty, he decided to get rid of her. This was easier said than done, since her nephew, Charles V, was Holy Roman Emperor and controlled the pope. Henry was therefore unable to dispose of his original dispensation and his reaction was to break off from Rome.

Henry's Reformation was a peculiarly English one. He despised the more extreme forms of Protestantism, as the reaction against the Catholic Church was known. The various kinds of Protestants agreed on only one thing – that Catholic doctrines based on Church teachings alone were inadmissible. Only the Bible contained the truth. Apart from that, as the ensuing wars of religion were to demonstrate many times, the Protestants were quite happy to kill one another as well as Catholics.

All of this seems strange to us centuries later; after all, one of the major Christian tenets is that one must never kill anyone. But politics was the major complicating factor. The combination excited passions in a way that had far-reaching effects.

Shakespeare's works were written during the reigns of Elizabeth and James, and show great awareness of the issues involved. Elizabeth attempted to tread a middle road between Catholicism and extreme Protestantism. But eventually the pope declared that it was perfectly legal for any Catholic to resist her policies, or even assassinate her. The links between religion and politics were strengthened as a result. English national pride in fact ensured that many Catholics did not resist their Queen, but the damage was done. The problem continued through the reign of James and into that of his son Charles. Here are several suggested texts:

- Eamon Duffy, *The Stripping of the Altars: Traditional religion in England, 1400 – 1580* (New Haven and London: Yale University Press, 1992)
- R.H. Tawney, *Religion and the Rise of Capitalism* (London: Peregrine Books, 1987)
- Keith Thomas, *Religion and the Decline of Magic* (London: Penguin Books, 1991)

Gender

Biological sex and gender are not the same thing. Think of gender as the ways in which society expects you to behave: it is socially constructed, and can vary across time and from culture to culture. For example, masculinity in ancient Greece, at least among the upper classes, was bisexual.

We have already touched upon gender differences. In the English Renaissance, men were considered superior. They were supposed to be active, forceful and outgoing. Women were considered weak and incapable of the same intellectual achievements as men. These are the terms on which Renaissance patriarchy was based.

Of course, since gender is socially constructed, patterns of behaviour are not necessarily fixed. This simple fact makes a nonsense of the claims of patriarchy. It is an ideology, not a science. The effects of these preconceptions on literature and drama, as well as politics, have become something of a growth industry in critical and historical work. More will be suggested in Chapter 8, since gender studies is a major critical movement in its own right. However, to start with, here are some suggestions for looking at how gender functioned in Shakespeare's time:

- Susan Dwyer Amussen, *An Ordered Society: Gender and Class in Early Modern England* (New York: Columbia University Press, 1988)
- Anne Laurence, *Women in England, 1500 – 1760: A Social History* (London: Orion Publishing Group, 1994)
- Lawrence Stone, *The Family, Sex and Marriage in England, 1500 – 1800* (London: Penguin Books, 1990)

Europe and Beyond

Queen Elizabeth's diplomacy was based on a balancing act, as we have already seen. The moment of crisis came in the 1580s, with the execution of Mary, Queen of Scots, and the defeat of the Spanish Armada. After this, the accession of James of Scotland was assured.

Strangely enough, James never showed any rancour towards Elizabeth for the execution of his mother. This can be explained partly through religion; James saw himself as a Protestant prince, while his politically inept mother was a strong adherent of Catholic France. Also, of course, by succeeding Elizabeth, James accomplished a long-cherished English ideal: the unification of the British Isles under one crown. Ireland, of course, was to suffer grievously as a result.

The reign of Elizabeth and the unification of the crowns brought the country's role into prominence; not only in relation to Europe, but also to the world as a whole. Trade and politics became inextricably mixed, if not indistinguishable. Here is some suggested reading:

- Perry Anderson, *Lineages of the Absolutist State* (London: Verso, 1993)
- Kenneth R. Andrews, *Trade, Plunder and Settlement: Maritime Enterprise and the Genesis of the British Empire, 1480 – 1630* (Cambridge: Cambridge University Press, 1984)
- Peter Hulme, *Colonial Encounters: Europe and the Native Caribbean, 1492 – 1797* (London and New York: Routledge, 1992)

Tutorial

Study tips

1 Before you start to study a play in earnest, as opposed simply to reading it over, try the following exercise: take six separate pieces of A4 paper, each headed with one of the sections from this chapter. As you go through the play, take notes according to which sections of the play seem to fit into any of the six categories. Although the play may not relate to all six, you should end up with a good idea of the areas in which you may need to do some further reading on contemporary issues. This can be a good way to approach exam revision as well as essay preparation.

2 If, following the exercise above, you find that more than one play seems to deal with the same issues, you are in a good position to exploit the plays as a pair or group. Many exams ask you to deal with more than one play in your answer: this is a shortcut to effective revision.

Discussion points

1 Pick two of the section titles above that seem most appropriate to the play you are to discuss. An example might be the roles of the head of state and religion in the figures of the Duke and Angelo in *Measure For Measure*. What does the conjunction of these two issues tell you about how the play relates to its immediate cultural context?

2 Do you see generic distinctions between which plays seem to pick up on which issues?

Practical assignments

1 Take advantage of television. Try to watch programmes that fall within the period of your course.

2 Go to the library and look at some historical atlases. You will find it easier to deal with political and historical movements if you are able to picture them in your mind's eye; an atlas can be an excellent visual aid.

Practice questions

1. How does a Shakespeare play take advantage of the dramatic form to enact contemporary social concerns?

2. How does Shakespeare address the anxieties of Renaissance England in plays set elsewhere, or in other times?

8 **Dealing with Critics**

One-minute overview

It is now time to decide what you want to do about the critics. Most introductory level courses will not expect you to deal with secondary critical material in depth. But if you can utilise criticism you will demonstrate an ability to integrate your own ideas with recognised wider issues. This can only have a beneficial effect on your grades, provided that you manage it appropriately. This chapter will introduce you to the major critical movements and provide you with ideas for further reading.

There will be sections on:
- Managing critics
- Liberal humanism
- Structuralism, deconstruction and post-structuralism
- Psychoanalysis
- Feminisms and gender
- New historicism
- Cultural materialism
- Performance
- Postmodernism and post-colonial theory

Managing Critics

The more intensive and advanced your engagement with Shakespeare, the more you will be expected to deal with criticism. Once again, this means that you will have to perform a balancing act. You will need to decide for yourself how much time and effort you can afford to devote to secondary material. The best basis on which to make this decision is cost effectiveness: how much effort will be needed to ensure a decent return on the investment of time and energy? If Shakespeare forms only a small part of your study, then by all means avoid the critics. If you feel the need to engage a little bit, then you will need to know at least the main positions adopted by different types of commentator. But if you wish to investigate their works in detail, you will have to learn how to distinguish between different viewpoints, as well as how to integrate them into your own work.

Basically, there are three responses to critics. There are those with whom you completely disagree. There are those with whom you agree. And then there are those you find useful, but only in a partial or limited manner. You then have to work out how to include material into your own written work. The easiest way is by means of reference. This is a common technique in exam situations, and also when you wish to characterise a writer's position without necessarily going to all the trouble of quoting from it. In such a case you would summarise the main points and then note them in your references. Always remember to do this – you don't want to be accused of passing off someone else's work as your own.

But how do you make quotations work for you? You need to make sure that you integrate them fully into your own argument. The best way is to use linking sentences before and after the quotation. These sentences mean nothing in and of themselves, but they join the quotations to your own text. They also subtly signal to your reader that not only have you understood this critic, but that you have found a quotation and you are using it effectively to supplement your own discussion.

You might be quoting a passage from a critic with whom you disagree. You would write a sentence introducing the quotation, then quote, and finally link it more fully with your own argument. Here is an example:

In his book (title) critic (name) discusses the balcony scene in *Romeo and Juliet* (II.ii) as follows:

Quote

However, this fails to take into account the performance circumstances of the Renaissance platform stage. Rather than follow this account, it is more fruitful to continue my argument...

You will notice that the linking sentences do not advance your argument. But they make sure that the quotation works for you. You want to avoid a situation in which you appear to be quoting merely for the sake of it, because you happen to have found a useful critical passage. Make the critics work for you!

Liberal Humanism

One thing you must remember is that all critics have an agenda, especially when they say they do not. One of the purposes of this chapter is to give you an idea of the different groups of critical approaches. This will help you to identify the kinds of interests of the various critics you will come across. You do not want to quote two critics positively, only to have marks deducted because you have not noticed that they violently disagree with each other.

The best group to start off with is that usually labelled as 'liberal humanist'. These are critics whose work is often quoted approvingly if only because they are very traditional in their approach. You may already have come across some of them. You will find them using terms such as 'human nature', 'timeless truths', 'the great genius of Shakespeare' and so on. They believe that Shakespeare's plays embody the imagination of the world's greatest literary figure, and that we can gain access to great truths about the human condition as a result. Any historical specifics are considered purely secondary to these transcendent insights. Representative texts include:

- Jonathan Bate, *The Genius of Shakespeare* (London: Picador, 1997)
- E.M.W. Tillyard, *Shakespeare's History Plays* (London: Penguin Classics, 1991)
- Stanley Wells, *Shakespeare: A Dramatic Life* (London: Sinclair-Stevenson, 1994)

Structuralism, Deconstruction and Post-Structuralism

As a critical movement, structuralism is most often associated with linguistics and anthropology. However, it had an effect on literary studies because of links with a group of critics known as the Russian Formalists. One of these, Roman Jakobson, became a major figure in linguistics, and also published literary criticism. Historically, it could be argued that structuralism emerges as part of the scientistic mood of the later 19th century, in which many other disciplines have their root. It is therefore the counterpart in language studies of sociology and psychology.

Jakobson left Russia in the aftermath of the 1917 Revolution and the ensuing Civil War. He united the work of the Formalists with the linguistics of Ferdinand de Saussure and corresponded closely with the founder of structural anthropology, Claude Levi-Strauss. Eventually this gave rise to the theories of narratology in the 1960s, which were mostly concerned with the short story and the novel.

Structuralism was therefore not closely involved with Shakespeare studies, although Jakobson did produce a detailed analysis of Shakespeare's Sonnet 129 in collaboration. However, the reaction against structuralism in the 1960s has produced two major movements in literary studies, namely deconstruction and post-structuralism. Jacques Derrida is crucial for the former, and Roland Barthes for the latter. These movements are not the same thing, and although this is not a book on literary theory, you still need to have some idea of how they relate to one another.

Many recent critics have been influenced by the successors to structuralism, especially in terms of their interests in how language works and in the stylistics of their own writing. This is extremely difficult material in its own right, and critics who utilise the various associated techniques can be very 'literary' in the styles they adopt in their analytical writing. As a result, however, their work can be liberating rather than frustrating. The emphasis on how language operates could well be something you might find useful and important for your own work. Here are some references to get you started:

- Catherine Belsey, 'Disrupting sexual difference: meaning and gender in the comedies', in John Drakakis (ed.), *Alternative Shakespeares* (London: Routledge, 1996, p.166ff)
- Terence Hawkes, *Meaning By Shakespeare* (London: Routledge, 1992)
- R. Jakobson and L.G. Jones, *Shakespeare's Verbal Art in Th'Expense of Spirit* (The Hague: Mouton, 1970)

Psychoanalysis

In a manner similar to liberal humanism, criticism influenced by psychoanalysis is also interested in what it sees as fundamental human truths. However, in this case the truths are those inherent to the human psyche itself, and literary texts are read and analysed for the insight they give both into the author's mind and into the way that the human mind operates in general, in accordance with Freudian theory. Later psychoanalytical work draws on Jacques Lacan's re-interpretation of Freud's ideas, and is heavily influenced by an approach similar to structuralism. As with some post-structuralist work, you will have to make yourself acquainted with the basic tenets of psychoanalytical theory in order to be able to follow the Shakespearean criticism. Here are some titles:

- Janet Adelman, *Suffocating Mothers: Fantasies of Maternal Origin in Shakespeare's Plays* (London and New York: Routledge, 1992)
- Murray M. Schwartz and Coppelia Kahn (eds), *Representing Shakespeare: New Psychoanalytic Essays* (Baltimore and London: Johns Hopkins University Press, 1980)

Feminisms and Gender

There are many different kinds of feminist criticism (hence the plural in this section's title). As far as Shakespeare studies is concerned, they range from an interest in female characters in the plays to analyses of gender roles. Also, feminist critics and gender theorists are very open to influences from groups such as those already discussed – you will probably have noticed already that some of the critics mentioned in previous sections are women, or are interested in gender issues. As with other suggestions in this chapter, the following list should give you a good place to start:

- Deborah E. Barker and Ivo Kamps (eds), *Shakespeare and Gender: A History* (London: Verso, 1995)
- Juliet Dusinberre, *Shakespeare and the Nature of Women* (London: Macmillan, 1996)
- Lorna Hutson, *The Usurer's Daughter: Male Friendship and Fictions of Women in Sixteenth-Century England* (London: Routledge, 1994)

New Historicism

This is a group of contemporary American critics. They have been heavily influenced by the French cultural theorist Michel Foucault, via anthropology. Their main interest is in the interplay of state power and cultural forms. Many of them see Shakespearean drama as reinforcing the norm, and their ideas are often couched in terms of a debate over subversion of dominant forms and the containment of these ideas. Examples include:

- Stephen J. Greenblatt, *Shakespearean Negotiations: The Circulation of Social Energy in Renaissance England* (Oxford: The Clarendon Press, 1992)
- Jean E. Howard and Marion F. O'Connor (eds), *Shakespeare Reproduced: The Text in History and Ideology* (New York and London: Methuen, 1987)
- Leonard Tennenhouse, *Power On Display* (New York and London: Methuen, 1986)

Cultural Materialism

Often confused with the American New Historicists, this is a group of British academics whose predecessor was the influential left-wing critic Raymond Williams. Their interest differs from that of the Americans in that they argue for a more complex analysis of texts that goes beyond the axis of subversion versus containment. They are also acutely aware of the differences between Shakespeare's times and our own, and thus are explicitly engaged in questions of historicity, interpretation and appropriation. Some sample texts are:

- Jonathan Dollimore and Alan Sinfield (eds), *Political Shakespeare: Essays in Cultural Materialism* (Manchester: Manchester University Press, 1996)
- Graham Holderness (ed.), *The Shakespeare Myth* (Manchester: Manchester University Press, 1988)
- Ivo Kamps (ed.), *Materialist Shakespeare: A History* (London: Verso, 1995)

Performance

There are various aspects to performance studies as they relate to Shakespeare. Plenty of material exists on modern performances of the plays, but there is not so much on the conditions of contemporary Renaissance performances. This last subject can be subdivided into critics who try to imagine the actual practices of the Renaissance stage, and those who produce work on the culture of the stage that is almost sociological. Here are some recommended texts:

- Andrew Gurr, *The Shakespearean Stage 1574–1642* (Cambridge: Cambridge University Press, 1995)
- Dennis Kennedy, *Looking At Shakespeare: A Visual History of Twentieth-Century Performance* (Cambridge: Cambridge University Press, 1996)
- Robert Weimann, *Shakespeare and the Popular Tradition in the Theater: Studies in the Social Dimension of Dramatic*

Form and Function (Baltimore and London: Johns Hopkins University Press, 1978)

- W.B. Worthen, *Shakespeare and the Authority of Performance* (Cambridge: Cambridge University Press, 1997)

Postmodernism and Post-Colonial Theory

Postmodernism is not the same as post-structuralism. It is an artistic movement that has arisen from a dissatisfaction with the monolothic forms associated with modernism. It takes the logic of reference beyond that of modernism, extending it to all areas of cultural production instead of only the elite. It has been accused of being all surface and no substance. In relation to Shakespeare studies it has opened up alternative areas of interest from those associated with more traditional viewpoints. The emphasis on alternatives has helped the growth of new modes of analysis such as post-colonial theory. The attempt to re-read Shakespeare plays from previously excluded perspectives has benefited as a result. Of course, that is not to say that only postmodernism has provided such an impetus. The Barker and Hulme essay mentioned below is avowedly materialist, as well as being one of the major post-colonial interventions. Here are some texts you might like to try:

- Francis Barker and Peter Hulme, 'Nymphs and reapers heavily vanish: the discursive con-texts of *The Tempest*' in John Drakakis (ed.), *Alternative Shakespeares* (London: Methuen, 1996)
- James C. Bulman (ed.), *Shakespeare, Theory, and Performance* (London and New York: Routledge, 1996)
- Ania Loomba and Martin Okrin (eds), *Post-Colonial Shakespeares* (London: Routledge, 1998)

Tutorial

Study tips

1. If you are studying a particular group of critics in depth, try to find out more about them in general to give yourself a context for their work on Shakespeare. There are many collections of essays and commentaries on different aspects of criticism. The way that a particular critic is associated with a specific movement is crucial.

2. Some critics are associated with more than one of these groupings. If a critic's name comes up in, for example, a collection of post-colonial essays as well as in his or her own right as a single author, there may be a linkage that will be useful to you in understanding how the various kinds of criticism relate to one another.

Discussion points

1. Take liberal humanism and one of the other kinds of criticism. How does the other one relate to or challenge the more traditional humanist one? This is an extremely important question: there are massive debates going on between various kinds of criticism, and you do not want to be caught out.

2. Take any two critical groups. Is there a possible connection between them? For example, does a new-historicist approach necessarily preclude a feminist analysis, or could the two be compatible? The more you are able to trace possible connections, the more you put yourself in control of how these groups relate.

Practical assignments

1. If you are trying to read up on secondary critical material for your own work, try comparing the critics. For example, if you have to write about a

specific play, read several essays by different writers. How do they compare? What are they looking for? What are their main interests when analysing the play? If you are able to answer these questions, you will be able to detect the agendas of the critics.

2 Take several of the approaches we have been discussing. Note how you think each of them would analyse a specific play. Which sections of the text do you think they would find useful for their purposes? Are there areas of common interest? Are there contradictions?

Practice questions

1 Is a liberal-humanist interest in timeless truths compatible with a thorough analysis of a Shakespearean text?

2 Would a re-reading of marginalised figures such as Caliban in *The Tempest* by alternative critical approaches change the meaning of the play for you, or do you think that it merely opens up some extra nuances of meaning?

3 Should feminist analysis be confined to discussions of female characters, or should the whole apparatus of gender be analysed more fully?

You will probably not come across Shakespeare's poetry until you take more advanced courses. If you are asked to read some of it early in your student career, the chances are that it will be a selection of the sonnets. This is especially true if Shakespeare is only a minor part of your initial curriculum of study. One of the advantages of studying the poetry is that you will not have to incorporate the whole extra area of performance. However, you will need to be aware of the conventions governing Renaissance poetry, and the ways in which Shakespeare relates to them.

This chapter will be divided up as follows:
- The Sonnets: overview
- The Sonnets: 1–17
- The Sonnets: The young man
- The Sonnets: The dark lady
- *Venus and Adonis*
- *The Rape of Lucrece*
- *A Lover's Complaint*
- *The Passionate Pilgrim*
- *The Phoenix and the Turtle*

The Sonnets: Overview

Many modern readers find these poems puzzling, for a number of reasons. They were first published in 1609, although at least some of them were written well before that date. There is no direct evidence that Shakespeare was associated with their publication. They are dedicated to a certain Mr W.H. and much critical ingenuity has been spent on trying to figure out who this might have been. The same goes for the identity of the young man to whom most of the poems are addressed – is he Mr W.H.? Also, the poems that come later in the collection are addressed to a powerful but troubling female figure, who seems to come between the poet and the young man. There are also some poems that refer to a poet who rivals Shakespeare for the patronage of the young man. Even the order in which the poems were published has been questioned.

Editions subsequent to that of 1609 changed the 'young man' sonnets to make them seem to have been written to a woman, and the true text was not restored until the 20th century. Anxiety about Shakespeare's sexuality and the ambivalence of his relationship with the young man has been common among critics.

The English Renaissance sonnet had a massive surge in popularity in the 1580s and 1590s, mainly because of the influence of Sir Philip Sidney's collection entitled *Astrophel and Stella*. The other major collection was Spenser's *Amoretti*, but many poets tried their hand at producing shorter collections. These tend to take the form of a sequential narrative of a love affair between the poet and a woman who is superior to him in some way, or at least unavailable, and who has to be won over to love him. The collection tells the story of this love affair, and many of them are simply known as sequences because of their straightforward narratives. However, not all collections follow this pattern, and Shakespeare's is one of the most well known of these, as you will have seen from the introductory comments made above.

The Sonnets: 1–17

The first 17 sonnets are usually taken as a group. They seem to be addressed to the same young man as numbers 18–126. In the first group, the poet exhorts the young man to marry, deploying a large number of arguments to do so. The basis of these poems is the young man's aristocratic status: he should do his duty to his noble family by marrying and begetting an heir to carry on the line. Shakespeare uses all of the standard associations of the aristocracy to try to get his message across, but ultimately he fails. The young man is simply too self-willed to accord with the poetry's version of what he should be doing. Many commentators believe these poems to have been written in about 1592, when the London theatres were closed due to the plague and Shakespeare was under the patronage of the Earl of Southampton.

The Sonnets: the Young Man

Sonnets 18–126 explore the nature of the young man's identity and personality, and how the poet relates to him. These are the poems that have occasioned much of the controversy outlined above. The problem seems to be that they are couched in the language of courtly love that is commonly associated with sonnet writing, and of course these are addressed to a man. But the presence of the rival poet in some of the later poems may indicate another possibility: that the love convention is being deployed in the interests of a patronage relationship. The term 'love' was certainly not restricted in the Renaissance to its modern association of a personal, mutual attraction. We have already noted how the post-Renaissance preoccupation with the individual may have distorted the meanings of Shakespeare's plays. Might the same process be at work in the reception of the sonnets? These poems were written 400 years ago: is it possible that semantic change might account for the modern fascination with Shakespeare's sexuality?

The Sonnets: the Dark Lady

Sonnets 127–152 are addressed to a mysterious woman, commonly known as the 'Dark Lady'. The final two sonnets are almost purely conventional. Shakespeare's Lady seems to be much more wilfully difficult even than the ladies of other sonnet sequences, so much so that at times the poet seems to be tortured by the relationship.

It might be fruitful to remember that representations of women in this period are heavily conditioned by long-standing conventions. In this respect, Shakespeare's Dark Lady may simply be his exploration of a set of well-known themes, albeit with a twist of unusual originality. But this is precisely what sonneteers were supposed to do: play with the conventions they inherited. Again, it may be misleading to think of these poems as recording a real set of events in an actual love affair. Even if you believe that they do, try to remember the sonnet tradition as you write. At least that way you will avoid making some wild assumptions and generalisations.

Venus and Adonis

Published in 1593, *Venus and Adonis* is dedicated to Henry Wriothesley, the Earl of Southampton. It therefore dates from roughly the same time as many of the sonnets to the young man. It is very highly literary, even self-consciously so. Its style and content are derived from a strand of Latin poetry most closely associated with Ovid. In this respect it is very similar to Christopher Marlowe's poem *Hero and Leander*, and it is possible that the two playwrights continued their friendly rivalry in poetic form as the theatres were closed due to the plague.

Venus and Adonis tells the story of the love goddess' attempt to seduce Adonis, who is killed while out hunting. The erotic story gives the poet an occasion to demonstrate his skill in the language of passion. He plays with the conventions and the poem delights in its portrayal of Venus as the older seductress of the untried young man. There are plenty of sexual jokes, turning on the way in which the Latin tradition contravenes the more usual love tradition associated with courtly poetry. In *Venus and Adonis*, it is the woman who is extremely active in pursuit of her love, hunting him just as he hunts wild animals. From your point of view as a student, there is much material to be gleaned from the way the poem plays with stereotypes of masculinity and femininity.

The Rape of Lucrece

Another poem dating from the time of Shakespeare's literary (as opposed to dramatic) output is *The Rape of Lucrece*. It was published a year after *Venus and Adonis*. The later poem is based on a story found in the part of the Roman historian Livy's work that deals with early Rome, as well as elements of Ovid and, perhaps, others. It is a more sombre work than the previous long poem, which is only to be expected from its subject matter. It deals with the Etruscan King Tarquin's rape of Lucrece, the chaste wife of the Roman noble Collatine. Her subsequent suicide precipitates the rise of Rome against Etruscan oppression. Here you will find a great deal of material linking associations of masculinity and femininity with pseudo-historical events. In other words, the poem examines how sexual politics and high politics interrelate.

A Lover's Complaint

All of the poetry we have discussed so far draws upon a familiarity with conventions, and *A Lover's Complaint* is no exception. The poem was published as a companion piece in the same volume as the sonnets, and it is not absolutely certain that it is by Shakespeare. However, the poem displays an awareness of intricate details of the courtly love tradition in a way that betrays similarities to the treatment of the same conventions in the sonnets. The story is straightforward enough, since it is the complaint of an abandoned lover about her seducer. She is especially critical of the techniques he used to win her heart, all of which are familiar motifs from the love tradition. The poem exposes courtly love – and this includes sonnets – for a sham; they are a fashionable pose, masking the true intentions of the man who utilises them. The poem is a mine of useful comments on the nature of love and sexual betrayal, and as such you will be able to employ it as a secondary source in relation to plays that deal with the same issues.

The Passionate Pilgrim

This is a rather fragmentary collection of material by various authors, published in 1599. Five of the poems are Shakespearean sonnets that appear elsewhere in his works: two are slightly different versions of sonnets 138 and 144, while the others had already been published as part of the play *Love's Labour's Lost*. Some of the other poems have been definitely attributed to other poets; the remainder of the 20 poems may well have been written by Shakespeare. What is important about this collection is that it has provided a rough date for at least some of the sonnets. The fact that this was published at all may be an indication of the popularity of Shakespeare's name, since a collection of this nature associated with him was obviously expected to make some money.

The Phoenix and the Turtle

This is a single poem, attributed to Shakespeare, which was included in a collection published in 1601. It is not an easy poem to read, partly because of the metre used but mainly because of the abstruse nature of the subject. The poem is mostly concerned with the emblematic function of the phoenix and the turtle, especially since they are combined in marriage. It consists of three sections, and overall constitutes a kind of meditation on the meaning of love.

Tutorial

Study tips

1 Poetry from a period so long ago can be very confusing. Take advantage of the conventions that form the background to the poems you are reading. Make a list of the various concepts that occur to you as you read the poems. This will help you order your thoughts as you begin to re-read them when preparing for assignments.

2 Poetry lacks the advantage of performance material to help you fix ideas in your mind. Here is a way to manipulate your study time. It uses the fact that memory works by association. Every time you study a single long poem, or a group of sonnets that seem to share the same features, listen to the same piece of music in the background. It does not matter what kind of music you use; ideally it should be something memorable but not intrusive. This technique works especially well for exam situations; by recalling the music, you can usually help yourself remember the main points of the poetry.

Discussion points

1 Considerations of gender are very important in many of Shakespeare's poems. Does his poetry reinforce conventional gender stereotypes, or do you think that it challenges them, or at least puts them in question?

2 The issue of agency is similarly crucial. What happens when the poems investigate the circumstances within which action takes place? Are the possibilities for action circumscribed by gender positions or social rank?

Practical assignments

1 If you are dealing with the sonnets, read some sonnets by other contemporary writers. You will soon build up a picture of the assumed conventions. This will enable you to decide for yourself how Shakespeare's poems relate to those conventions.

2 You can use the same technique for the other poems. For example, you could read Marlowe's *Hero and Leander* as a point of comparison with *Venus and Adonis*. It is also a good idea to read some secondary material about classical influences on English Renaissance poetry.

Practice questions

1 'The ways in which Shakespeare's poems relate to Renaissance poetic conventions are at least as important as the ways that the plays are structured according to dramatic conventions.' Discuss.

2 Has the post-Renaissance preoccupation with the individual altered the perception of the meanings of Shakespeare's poetry?

Unlike all of the previous chapters, this one does not have a tutorial section. Instead, it is in itself a compilation of resource material that you might find useful. In addition to the further reading you will have found in chapters 7 and 8, there are some more generalised suggestions of books that are not so closely tied to specific schools of criticism. There are also some sample assessments and a review of some of the more interesting and useful websites.

The chapter has the following sections:
- Sample essay questions
- Sample exam paper
- Further reading
- Reviewed Shakespeare websites

Sample Essay Questions

1. *A Midsummer Night's Dream* and *Much Ado About Nothing* share several common interests. Both contain unpleasant events and yet are classed as comedies because of their endings. Do you see fundamental differences between these plays or are they closely related?
2. *Julius Caesar, Macbeth* and *A Midsummer Night's Dream* all rely heavily on supernatural elements. Choose two of them and discuss how each play integrates these issues into the action. Are they both successful, or does one play succeed where the other fails?
3. Discuss in detail how *Romeo and Juliet* and *Much Ado About Nothing* both deal with personal love and its social environment.
4. Choose two plays from *Julius Caesar, Macbeth* and *Romeo and Juliet*. Are both your plays tragedies of fate and chance?

5. *Macbeth, Henry IV part I, Henry V* and *Julius Caesar* are all heavily engaged with kingship and power. Analyse how two of these plays deal with these issues.

6. Does the jolly Prince Hal of *Henry IV part I* change smoothly into the powerful King of *Henry V*, or are there contradictions?

Sample Exam Paper

1. Investigate the ways in which the plays of your choice deal with questions of state power.

2. Discuss how social conflict is dramatised: are newly emerging concerns opposed to an established view of the world?

3. Analyse the relationship between the social worlds of your chosen plays and their main protagonists.

4. How do the plays you have studied reformulate prior historical events?

5. Discuss how the plays use contrasting social groups for dramatic effect.

6. How do the plays you have studied deal with gender power relations?

7. Give examples of how Shakespeare's plays set up interaction between characters.

8. How might Shakespeare's plays be analysed in terms of the staging constraints and conventions of his period?

9. Is the use of mixed genres confusing?

Further Reading

This list is comprised of books that deal with more than one text. They are either collections of essays or are explicitly concerned with a specific group of Shakespeare's plays. They have therefore been carefully chosen because they are suited to student requirements.

- Graham Holderness, *Shakespeare: The Histories* (London: Macmillan, 2000)

- Jean E. Howard and Phyllis Racken, *Engendering A Nation: A Feminist Account of Shakespeare's English Histories* (London and New York: Routledge, 1997)
- Coppelia Kahn, *Roman Shakespeare: Warriors, Wounds and Women* (London: Routledge, 1997)
- Victor Kiernan, *Eight Tragedies of Shakespeare* (London and New York: Verso, 1996)
- Simon Palfrey, *Late Shakespeare: A New World of Words* (Oxford: Clarendon Press, 1999)
- Jennifer Richards and James Knowles, (eds), *Shakespeare's Late Plays: New Readings* (Edinburgh: Edinburgh University Press, 1999)
- Peter Saccio, *Shakespeare's English Kings: History, Chronicle, and Drama* (Oxford: Oxford University Press, 1977)
- Vivian Thomas, *The Moral Universe of Shakespeare's Problem Plays* (London: Routledge, 1991)

There are also several series of essay collections available. For Shakespeare studies try the Longman Critical readers, the Icon Guides, the Casebooks and the New Casebooks. As with the titles given above, these series contain books that either range over specific groups of the plays or contain a selection of essays all on the same play. The editorial introductions and comments can be quite useful in describing the various critical approaches represented in the collections.

Reviewed Shakespeare Websites

There is no space here simply to list all of the websites devoted to Shakespeare. Nor would this serve any useful purpose. First of all, you can easily find the sites using any search engine. But secondly, most of them are – from the point of view of the student – rather useless. They tend to be engaged in displaying things such as 'sonnet of the day'. This might be of interest to the casual Shakespeare fan, but it is not going to help you with essay material.

Instead, here is a short list of the most useful sites from a student's perspective. You can easily follow the links to other sites that may be of specific interest to you, but this will depend on your precise needs at the time.

- *www.shakespeare.com*
- *www.bardware.com*
- *www.members.aol.com/EngShakes*
  This is the website of the English Shakespeare Company.
- *shakespeare.palomar.edu*
  This is a good guide to internet resources on Shakespeare.
- *www.bardweb.net*
  Another good guide to online resources.
- *www.shakespearemag.blogspot.com*
  Good for current news and links.

11

Course Materials: A Midsummer Night's Dream

One-minute overview

This is the first chapter containing material specific to one play. *A Midsummer Night's Dream* is one of the most commonly studied of Shakespeare's plays, so it makes sense to begin the chapters of course materials with it. The format of all of these chapters is the same, but this play lends itself most easily to the procedure I have adopted. You may of course not need to look at the others, but this one will give you a flavour of course handouts in their most accessible form.

This chapter contains:

■ A breakdown of the entire play, divided by act and scene
■ Discussion points

Play Breakdown

I.i.

1–19:	Theseus and Hippolyta on marriage: from war to revelry.
20–45:	Enter Egeus, Hermia, Lysander and Demetrius. Note especially Egeus' speech: marriage, patriarchy and force.
46–52:	Theseus' response.
53–64:	Theseus and Hermia.
65–90:	Theseus' judgement and Hermia's response.
91–98:	Demetrius vs. Lysander; love vs. family.
99–110:	Lysander's speech: money and worth. Note reference to Demetrius' inconstancy.

111–127:   Theseus responds. They all leave, except Lysander and Hermia.
128–179:   They discuss their predicament and decide to elope. Note the vocabulary of love and fate.
180–193:   Helena enters and speaks out against Hermia's beauty.
194–201:   Stychomachia: Hermia vs. Helena.
202–225:   Hermia and Lysander try to comfort Helena. Lysander tells her about their planned elopement. They then leave her alone.
226–251:   Helena's soliloquy.

I.ii.

1–69:   The 'actors' all enter. Prose.
70–78:   On the nature of theatrical illusion.
79–111:   They sort out their parts, then agree to meet in the forest at the Duke's oak.

II.i.

1–59:   Puck and a fairy enter separately. Conversation between them sets up their world, and the theme of separation.
60–145:   Both fairy monarchs enter separately with their courts. Extreme verbal violence and then Titania leaves with her attendants.
146–176: Oberon describes the plant he wants, then orders Puck to go and get it. Puck leaves.
176–187: Oberon's soliloquy. He retires, invisible, to watch the Athenians. Simultaneous staging unites the two worlds of the real and the fairy, at least visually.
187–242: Helena and Demetrius enter, watched by Oberon. Active woman, passive man as Helena woos Demetrius. He leaves, with Helena in hot pursuit.
243–268: Oberon decides to make Demetrius love Helena. Puck returns with the plant; Oberon takes some and orders Puck to put the juice on the Athenian man's eyes. They leave.

II.ii.

1–26:	Titania and her court. Various bits of 'niceness', then Titania goes to sleep with one fairy on guard duty.
27–34:	Oberon comes in unseen, squeezes the juice on Titania's eyes, then leaves again.
35–65:	Lysander and Hermia enter; zonal staging very common from here on, as they do not see Titania. They also go to sleep.
66–83:	Puck enters, squeezes juice onto Lysander's eyes, then leaves.
84–110:	Demetrius comes in, still pursued by Helena. More verbal violence and then he leaves, exasperated. Helena then awakens Lysander, who falls in love with her when he sees her; note 'sake... awake' rhyme here, and the emphasis on dreaming.
111–144:	Lysander professes love to Helena, who thinks he's making fun of her. She leaves in a foul mood, pursued by Lysander.
145–156:	Hermia wakes, frightened by an appropriate dream, and then goes off to find Lysander.

III.i.

1–76:	Prose as the 'actors' enter. Emphasis on the stage.
77–88:	Puck comes in and comments as audience; actor reference. Bottom goes off, followed by Puck; note his comment to the audience at this point.
89–102:	Shift to verse as the others practise. Note comment on men acting women's parts.
103–119:	Puck and Bottom come in and Bottom's new appearance scares off his friends. Lots of confused movement here as they all run off; Puck leaves as well. Bottom stays behind, not realising what has happened to him.

120–129:   Bottom on his own. Titania wakes up and falls in love with him.

130–162:   Titania and Bottom: satire on love language. She calls in her attendants.

163–201:   Interplay between the fairies and Bottom. They all leave together.

III.ii.

1–5:   Oberon is beginning to wonder what's been happening. Loss of control?

6–40:   Puck reports success with both Titania and the Athenian man.

41–81:   Demetrius and Helena enter and have a fight as Oberon and Puck watch. Hermia leaves.

82–87:   Demetrius gives up the chase and goes to sleep.

88–101:   Oberon realises what has happened. Puck leaves.

102–109:   Oberon's verse as he charms Demetrius. Puck returns.

110–121:   Puck's comments; he's enjoying the confusion. Helena and Lysander enter, having been drawn here by Puck.

122–136:   Fight between Helena and Lysander.

137–176:   Demetrius wakes up and falls in love with Helena. Both men now woo her. She is utterly exasperated, convinced that they're both making fun of her.

177–344:   Hermia comes in and there's lots of confusion, almost coming to blows. Eventually they all leave in different directions.

345–395:   Oberon decides to sort it all out, orders Puck to do so, then leaves.

395–463:   Puck leads them all in, one after the other, puts them to sleep and uses the juice appropriately to set everything to rights – except for Demetrius.

IV.i.

1–45:	Lots of fun as Titania plays with Bottom in front of her court, all the time being watched by the invisible Oberon. Eventually the court leaves and Titania and Bottom fall asleep together.
46–75:	Puck enters and Oberon comes into the open. He uses the juice on Titania and then wakes her up.
76–102:	Reconciliation and the fairy world rejoices. They all leave except Bottom.
103–127:	Theseus, Hippolyta and the court all enter. Satire on the hunt. Note Theseus' language when he spots the four lovers.
128–138:	Various comments, then Theseus wakes them up.
139–186:	Marriages are arranged and Egeus is appeased. They all leave, except the lovers.
187–199:	The lovers talk, perplexed, then leave.
200–219:	Prose. Bottom's dream.

IV.ii

1–24:	The 'actors' enter, looking for Bottom.
25–45:	Bottom arrives and they all leave for the palace.

V.i.

1:	The court enters, apart from the lovers (who are offstage getting married at this point).
2–22:	Theseus' speech on imagination.
23–27:	Hippolyta's response.
27–107:	The two newly married couples enter, and all chat as the festivities are organised.
108–370:	Pyramus and Thisbe, with comments. Everyone goes off to bed.
371–390:	Puck enters and prepares the way for the fairy court.
391–422:	The fairy court enters, delivers its blessings, then leaves.
423–438:	Puck's epilogue. Acting.

Discussion Points

1. Marriage and love.

2. Acting and theatrical illusion.

3. Three worlds: Athens, the supernatural, and the forest in-between.

12

Course Materials: *The Tempest*

One-minute overview

This chapter repeats the techniques used in Chapter 11, but with reference to *The Tempest*. This is a very different play from *A Midsummer Night's Dream*, both in terms of its generic characteristics and the point in Shakespeare's career at which it was produced. The two plays have some things in common, notably elements of the supernatural, but the prime agent in the later play is a human being. If you are reading these chapters in sequence, you should be able to pick out points of comparison and contrast that will stand you in good stead when it comes to writing an essay about both.

This chapter has:

- ■ A breakdown of the entire play, divided by act and scene
- ■ Discussion points

Play Breakdown

I.i

1–4:	Prose conversation between the Shipmaster and the Boatswain. The Master tells the Boatswain to organise the mariners in order to deal with the great storm.
5–9:	The mariners enter and are given orders by the Boatswain.
10–27:	The courtiers enter and get in the way. The Boatswain treats them with contempt, then leaves.
28–33:	Gonzalo comments and then everyone leaves the stage: emphasis on chaotic movement here.

34–37:	The Boatswain.
38–50:	The courtiers re-enter: more verbal fighting between them and the Boatswain.
51–68:	Mariners enter, soaking wet; everyone gets ready for the shipwreck.

I.ii.

1–186:	Miranda asks Prospero to stop the storm; he tells her why he has raised it and links it to their own history, which he now finally explains to her. She falls asleep.
187–241:	Prospero is in command and Ariel reports what has happened. Offstage representation here.
242–299:	Ariel is recalcitrant; this gives Prospero the opportunity for another history lesson. They are reconciled.
300–304:	More orders from Prospero and Ariel leaves.
305–316:	Miranda wakes and she and her father discuss the household tasks. Caliban is also mentioned.
316:	Prospero calls on Caliban.
316–319:	Ariel reappears, is given secret instructions and then leaves again.
320:	Prospero 'conjures' Caliban to come in.
321–374:	Verbal violence between the three of them. Eventually, after threats, Caliban goes off to work.
375–408:	Ariel enters, leading Ferdinand by song.
409–503:	Ferdinand and Miranda fall in love, but Ferdinand is forced to work by Prospero, who magically stops him from attacking. Note various asides by Prospero.

II.i.

1–184:	The courtiers' differing descriptions of the island. Some of their recent history is explained.
185–198:	Ariel enters, starts putting some of the courtiers to sleep, then leaves.
199–296:	Antonio persuades Sebastian to kill his brother.

297–327:   Ariel comes back in time to forestall the assassination. With everyone awake, they all move further on in to the island.

II.ii.

1–14:   Caliban's soliloquy.

14–17:   Caliban sees Trinculo come in, mistakes him for one of Prospero's agents and tries to avoid being punished.

18–41:   Trinculo's description of the island, the storm and Caliban. He takes shelter.

42–55:   Stephano enters, drunk.

56–187:   Interplay between the three, including Stephano's description of Caliban.

III.i.

1–15:   Ferdinand's soliloquy as he works.

15–91:   Miranda enters, followed by Prospero, who remains unseen. She and Ferdinand express their love for each other, watched by her father. The two younger people then leave separately.

92–96:   Prospero speaks directly to the audience.

III.ii.

1–40:   More interplay between Caliban, Trinculo and Stephano.

41–145:   Ariel enters unseen. The three discuss murdering Prospero as Ariel plays music.

146–152:   They discuss matters some more, then go off to kill Prospero.

III.iii.

1–17:   The courtiers are having problems with the island.

18–52:   Prospero enters, in control and unseen by the courtiers. Dancing and music accompany the placing of a grand feast before the courtiers. Note Prospero's various asides.

53–82:	Ariel, in the likeness of a harpy, disrupts everything and magically charms the courtiers. Ariel then delivers a history of their deeds, and the dinner vanishes before their eyes.
83–93:	Prospero comments on all of this to the audience, then leaves.
94–109:	Various confused responses and exits from the courtiers.

IV.i.

1–33:	Prospero's reconciliation with Ferdinand and Miranda.
34–50:	Prospero gives more orders to Ariel, who leaves.
51–59:	Preparations for the masque.
60–138:	The wedding masque.
139–163:	Prospero stops the entertainment and gives spurious reasons to the couple, who then leave.
164–187:	Ariel re-enters. Prospero gives very precise instructions and Ariel leaves to carry them out.
188–193:	Prospero's comments on Caliban.
193:	Ariel enters with various beautiful costumes.
194–254:	Caliban, Trinculo and Stephano come in. Caliban keeps their intentions in mind, but the others are seduced by the trappings Ariel has left.
255–266:	The Wild Hunt as anti-masque drives them off the stage.

V.i.

1–32:	Prospero in full power. Discussion with Ariel, who goes off to bring in the various characters.
33–57:	Prospero's speech on his art and his renouncing of it.
58–103:	The courtiers are brought in by Ariel and judged by Prospero. Ariel goes off to fetch the mariners.
104–171:	Prospero continues with the courtiers.
172–215:	Ferdinand and Miranda are revealed, playing chess. Mass reconciliation.

215–255:   The mariners are led in by Ariel; note the asides between Ariel and Prospero as more reconciliations take place.

256–319:   Caliban, Trinculo and Stephano also come on. Comments and finale; note that the entire cast is on stage at this point. Everyone leaves except Prospero.

Epilogue

1–20:   Prospero's epilogue.

Discussion Points

1. Social rank and politics.

2. The supernatural.

3. Colonisation.

4. Gender and innocence.

13

Course Materials: *Romeo and Juliet*

One-minute overview

The play breakdown included in this chapter is more complex than the previous two. This is in order to pay as much attention as possible to the staging conventions of the Renaissance, as well as important thematic issues.

The chapter contains:
- A breakdown of the entire play, divided by act and scene
- Discussion points

Play Breakdown

Prologue

1–14:	Sonnet-form description of what is going to happen; sets up dramatic irony from the outset. Important vocabulary of fate and of acting.

I.i.

1–33:	Samson and Gregory, two Capulet servants, enter in mid-conversation. They set up the context of the feud between the Capulets and Montagues.
34–58:	Enter Abram and Balthasar, two Montague servants. Vicious insults are thrown at them by the Capulet servants.
59–72:	Enter Benvolio (note his name; at several points he tries to act as the voice of calmness). He attempts to stop a fight breaking out. Enter Tybalt; lots of fighting. Note the staging of his mistake; he thinks that Benvolio has drawn his sword in order to make the odds favour the

Montagues. He does not stop to think about the situation.

73–74: Enter the neutral citizens, who try either to stop the fight or to destroy both parties.

75–80: Enter both leaders and their wives; both men want to join in the fight.

81–103: Enter Prince Escalus and servants. Peace enforced; the Prince lays down the law. Everyone leaves, except the Montagues and Benvolio.

104–115: Benvolio describes what happened; his narrative accords with what the audience has seen, thus reinforcing his role as truthful voice of reason.

116–155: Descriptions of Romeo, whom the audience has not yet seen.

156–159: Romeo enters and Benvolio decides to try to find out what is wrong with him. Romeo's parents leave.

160–238: Game of wit between Romeo and Benvolio. Note the conventional language of love used by Romeo.

I.ii.

1–37: Enter Capulet, Paris and a servant. Again, staged as though in mid-conversation. Paris and Capulet begin by talking about the fight, but then move on to the matter of marriage between Paris and Juliet. Note Capulet's reference to her love being important; later the audience learns that this does not even remotely matter. Also note that from line 10 the discussion takes place in rhyming couplets: a sign of the sheer conventionality of what is being discussed. Narrative patterning: as with Romeo, Juliet is described before the audience actually sees her.

38–44: Paris and Capulet leave. The servant describes his orders to get things ready for the feast; he is, of course, illiterate. Note the switch to prose here.

45–56:	Enter Romeo and Benvolio. More witty banter, then they notice the servant.
57–81:	Conversation between Romeo and the servant; this is when Romeo learns of the feast at Capulet's house. The servant leaves.
82–101:	Benvolio and Romeo discuss attending the feast, primarily because of the presence of Rosaline, the woman Romeo thinks he loves. Again, note his love language here.

I.iii.

1–4:	Relations between Lady Capulet and Juliet's Nurse.
5–99:	Enter Juliet. Relations between the three women, especially on the subject of marriage. Note the vocabulary of books in Lady Capulet's description of Paris (79–94).
100–105:	Enter a serving man; preparations for the feast.

I.iv.

1–52:	The Montague youths and their conversation, especially a duel of word-play between Romeo and Mercutio.
53–95:	Mercutio's 'Queen Mab' speech.
95–114:	More general conversation, during which Romeo refers to fate.

I.v.

1–15:	Capulet servants prepare the feast; note change to prose here. Simultaneous staging.
16–40:	The Capulets enter with their guests. Big party.
41–92:	Multiple simultaneous staging of the feast, Romeo's observations and Tybalt's conversation with Capulet. Tybalt leaves rather than cause a fight.
93–110:	Mutual sonnet between Romeo and Juliet. They are interrupted by the Nurse.

111–117:	Romeo finds out from the Nurse who Juliet is. Note line break in 116.
117–118:	Romeo aside.
119–127:	The party finishes and everyone leaves except Juliet and the Nurse. The audience never finds out what Benvolio whispers to Capulet; playing with suspense and audience expectations.
128–145:	Juliet finds out through the Nurse who Romeo is.

II: Prologue

1–14:	Sonnet form.

II.i.

1–2:	Romeo enters alone, then withdraws. Zonal staging.
3–42:	Benvolio and Mercutio look for Romeo. Mercutio satirises Romeo's conventional love poses.

II.ii.

1:	Romeo's comment on Mercutio.
2–25:	Romeo's description of Juliet. Multiple line breaks in line 25.
26–49:	Romeo's comments are followed by Juliet's speech, with Romeo's aside.
49–135:	Their conversation, with mutual declarations of love. Interrupted by the Nurse calling offstage.
136–185:	Multiple movements by Juliet onstage and offstage.
186–189:	Romeo's final comments.

II.iii.

1–30:	Friar Laurence's soliloquy. Important vocabulary of decay, with its obvious metaphorical commentary on the plot intensified by Romeo's entrance.

31–94:   Conversation, with Laurence's sharp comments on Romeo's 'love' for Rosaline. Note the rhyming couplets as a sign of conventional wisdom; although they both use them, Romeo employs enjambement more often.

II.iv.

1–35:   Benvolio and Mercutio again. Note the change to prose here.

36–101:   Enter Romeo; sharp jesting word play, especially between Romeo and Mercutio. Obvious dramatic irony at line 87.

101–144: Nurse and Peter enter; she becomes the object of Mercutio's satire. Benvolio and Mercutio leave.

145–216: Conversation between Romeo and the Nurse.

II.v.

1–17:   Juliet's soliloquy.

18–20:   Her welcome to the Nurse. Peter leaves.

21–78:   Conversation. Nurse plays with delay, e.g. by using monosyllables. Note Juliet's exclamation to fate.

II.vi.

1–15:   Conversation between Romeo and Friar Laurence.

16–37:   Juliet enters. Note that the marriage is prefigured, not actually staged.

III.i.

1–34:   Various Montagues together, including Benvolio and Mercutio. Interplay between these two: moderation versus hotheaded wit.

35–55:   Enter the equivalent Capulets, including Petruchio and Tybalt. Obvious patterning here. Verbal sparring between Mercutio and Tybalt; Benvolio as the voice of wisdom.

56–120: Romeo enters and things explode. Tybalt tries to provoke Romeo, but he constantly attempts to keep the peace. Tybalt and Mercutio fight and Mercutio is fatally wounded when Romeo tries to break it up. A great deal of movement, although Mercutio dies offstage.

121–136: Romeo kills Tybalt when he hears of Mercutio's death; he then leaves on Benvolio's advice.

137–140: The citizens come in and try to work out who has killed whom; a great deal of confusion.

141–197: The Prince and both parties enter; Benvolio recounts the events truthfully. Romeo is banished.

III.ii.

1–31: Juliet's soliloquy in her happiness; obvious dramatic irony.

32–35: Nurse enters; Juliet immediately knows something is wrong.

36–143: Their conversation. Note the vocabulary of love employed by Juliet.

III.iii.

1–80: Romeo and Friar Laurence, balancing III.ii.36–143 above. Note Romeo's vocabulary of love.

81–175: Nurse enters, and the three discuss what is to be done. Note Romeo's talk of suicide; the Friar stops him.

III.iv.

1–35: Juliet's parents and Paris. Note the reality of arranged marriage from line 12, rather than the empty rhetoric of I.ii.1–37.

III.v.

1–59: Romeo and Juliet's morning after. Interrupted by the Nurse with news that Juliet's mother is on her way. Romeo leaves.

60–64:   Juliet's comments on fate.

64–103:   Juliet and her mother.

104–115: Juliet is informed about her marriage.

116–123: Her response.

124–125: Her mother invokes the name of the father.

126–195: Capulet enters along with the nurse; his discourse on the brutal facts of marriage under patriarchy. He then leaves in a rage.

196–201: Juliet appeals to her mother.

202–203: Lady Capulet's refusal and exit.

204–234: Nurse and Juliet; Nurse's advice rejected.

235–242: Juliet's soliloquy.

IV.i.

1–17:   Paris and Friar Laurence; Laurence takes Juliet's side. Note his reasons, as well as the obvious dramatic irony.

18–43:   Juliet enters. Three-way spat played very quickly with short lines. Paris on love.

44–126:   Paris leaves while Juliet laments. Note narrative patterning of her talk on suicide. Friar Laurence's remedy.

IV.ii.

1–14:   Capulet household preparing for the wedding regardless of Juliet's previous objections.

15–22:   Enter Juliet; dramatic irony of her submission.

23–37:   Capulet's response. Juliet and Nurse leave.

38–47:   Conversation between the parents.

IV.iii.

1–5:   Juliet asks the Nurse to leave her alone that night.

6–13:   Lady Capulet enters and offers to help with the wedding preparations. First time she has ever thought of Juliet in 14 years?

14–58:   The others leave; Juliet's soliloquy. Reference to acting at line 19. She drinks the potion.

IV.iv.

1–28:   A great deal of movement as the Capulet household prepares for the wedding. Dramatic irony of the contrast between all this movement and the audience's knowledge of the stillness of Juliet's 'death'. Note that it is the Nurse who goes to fetch her for the wedding.

IV.v.

1–16:   Staging of the Nurse's discovery.

17–32: Multiple stagings of discovery as various people arrive separately. Note Capulet's selfish language.

33–64: Mourning.

65–95: Friar Laurence's sermon attacks the Capulets. Everyone leaves except the Nurse and musicians.

96–99: Short conversation between the Nurse and the musicians. Note the playing with audience expectations and knowledge at line 99. Nurse leaves and Peter enters.

100–146: Prose. Minor characters used as chorus to the action, and some foolery to ease the tension.

V.i.

1–11:   Romeo's soliloquy balances Juliet's at beginning of III.iii; so does the dramatic irony.

12–33: Balthasar enters with the wrong news. Note vocabulary of fate in Romeo's response. Balthasar exits.

34–56: Romeo's soliloquy.

56–86: Apothecary enters in response to Romeo's shouting. Romeo buys the poison; obvious parallel with Juliet's 'poison'.

V.ii.

1–30:   The two friars; letter to Romeo not delivered. Laurence tries to forestall misfortune by preparing to visit Juliet's tomb.

V.iii.

1–21:   Paris and his page. Attempt to get some audience sympathy for Paris before his unlucky death?

22–73:   Romeo and Balthasar enter. Note patterning between both pairs. Romeo kills Paris.

74–120: Romeo's soliloquy and death.

121–147: Friar Laurence arrives and converses with Balthasar.

148–159: Laurence and Juliet: fate. Laurence leaves in fear.

160–170: Juliet's soliloquy and death.

171–310: Multiple staging of the discoveries of the two deaths. See especially Laurence's explanation. Prince's choral function at end.

Discussion Points

1. Kind of acting. Textual references to acting. Zonal staging and use of asides and soliloquies.
2. Staging techniques: choreography, offstage action and use of props, etc.
3. Changes in scenes: short scenes to long; poetry to prose; beginnings of the scenes.
4. The play's use of fate and the interplay with dramatic irony. Manipulations of audience expectations.
5. Patternings between the figures of Romeo and Juliet and their relationship to the world they live in. Why does the audience almost never see Romeo's family life, while Juliet's is very important in the plot development? Why does Romeo have friends outside his immediate family, while Juliet doesn't?
6. Discourses of love, especially conventional ones.

14

Course Materials: *King Lear*

One-minute overview

The play breakdown in this chapter is longer and more complex than the previous ones. This is partly because it is not easy for students to deal with *King Lear* early on in higher education. This chapter will also be useful for tutors, since the information is so comprehensive.

In this chapter you will find:
- A breakdown of the entire play, divided by act and scene
- Discussion points

Play Breakdown

I.i.

1–33:	Conversation between Edmund, Kent and Gloucester in prose. Begins in mid-flow, with an immediate reference to potential differences in the King's treatment of some of the higher nobility. Also sets up the current court as a kind of feudalism, especially with regard to the issue of illegitimacy. Edmund's response is important.
34–35:	The rest of the court enters and the play switches to poetry. Gloucester and Edmund leave in order to attend the King of France and the Duke of Burgundy. Lear describes his decision to split the kingdom; notice the use of the Royal 'we'.
45:	Lear talks to Cornwall and Albany.
45–54:	Lear on love; reference to the presence of the King of France and the Duke of Burgundy in competition for marriage to Lear's youngest daughter. Lear asks Goneril to speak.

55–61:	Goneril's response: use of rhetoric.
62:	Cordelia aside.
63–67:	Lear rewards Goneril.
67–68:	Lear asks Regan to speak.
69–76:	Regan's response, using the same kind of rhetoric as Goneril. Regan describes herself as being very similar to Goneril; this will be developed further later on.
76–78:	Cordelia aside: reference to the Griselda story.
79–82:	Lear rewards Regan.
82–86:	Lear asks Cordelia to speak.
87–101:	Her response and Lear's repeated questions.
108–120:	Lear's decision to renounce her; note the vocabulary he uses.
120:	Kent interrupts.
121–139:	Lear announces his retirement in full.
139–187:	Kent's advice and Lear's response to it: Kent is banished. He leaves.
188–208:	France and Burgundy enter with their attendants and Gloucester. Lear and Burgundy talk about Cordelia.
208–213:	Lear talks to France about her as well.
213–223:	France's response replicates Kent's misgivings. This is an important criticism, since it comes from a fellow king.
223–233:	Cordelia speaks.
233–234:	Lear's response.
235–247:	France and Burgundy talk to each other about Cordelia; Burgundy decides to withdraw his suit because of the lack of a proper dowry.
247–249:	Cordelia's sarcasm toward Burgundy.
250–261:	France recognises Cordelia's worth (virtue?) and proposes marriage regardless of her situation.
262–266:	Lear's graceless response. Most of the court exits.
266–282:	The three sisters take their leave of one another. Cordelia is clearly in opposition to the other two: note especially her ability to see

through their words of love. She leaves with the King of France.

283–308: Prose discussion between Goneril and Regan. They already intend to use their newfound power, especially over the King their father.

I.ii.

1–22: Edmund's nature speech. This doubles as a Machiavellian soliloquy.

23–26: Switch to prose. Gloucester enters talking to himself about the changes at court.

26–45: Conversation between the two; Edmund's use of a forged letter.

46–58: Gloucester reads the letter and worries about it.

59–117: More conversation. Gloucester tells Edmund to find out more about his brother's possible treachery and then leaves, muttering about signs and portents (traditionally, these signified some turmoil in the state).

117–133: Edmund in soliloquy. He dismisses his father's superstition with a typically Machiavellian rational logic.

134–178: Edgar enters and is manipulated by Edmund. Note Edmund's reference to acting as his brother comes onstage. Edgar leaves, worried.

179–184: Edmund switches to a standard Machiavellian soliloquy in poetry.

I.iii.

1–26: Important conversation between Goneril and her steward Oswald. Begins with the first reference to the Fool, and ends up with Goneril acting on her previous conversation with Regan. As far as she is concerned, stirring up trouble would be a good idea.

I.iv.

1–7: Kent enters in disguise and delivers a short speech in poetry.

8–43:	Lear's 'court' enters and the action switches to prose. Lear and the unrecognised Kent have a conversation, which ends with Lear hiring him.
44–45:	Oswald enters and Lear attempts to talk to him; the steward snubs him and leaves.
46–77:	Lear and one of his knights talk about relations between Lear and Goneril.
78–94:	Oswald re-enters and is verbally assaulted by Lear; note Oswald's definition of Lear at line 64. Lear and Kent beat up Oswald and shove him offstage. Lear rewards Kent.
95–188:	The Fool enters: why at this point precisely? Important conversation between Lear, Kent and the Fool.
189–200:	Goneril enters and Lear asks her why she is angry. The Fool comments acidly on why Lear should even care.
201–217:	Goneril switches to poetry: obvious implications. She starts to overrule Lear. Note the Fool's comments.
218–235:	Lear starts to go mad and the Fool continues his running commentary on the action.
237–261:	Goneril pronounces her decision and completely overrules her father. Note the vicious and monstrous vocabulary of Lear's response. Poor Albany enters in the middle of this tirade and doesn't have a clue what is going on.
262–289:	Lear's two horrible speeches as he curses Goneril. Albany interjects uselessly. Lear exits.
290–293:	Albany asks Goneril what is going on. She doesn't even bother to give a full answer.
294–310:	Lear comes back on, storming about losing half of his followers. Albany asks him what he is talking about, and Lear responds by cursing Goneril in even more vicious language than before. He then storms out, this time for good.
310–321:	Albany and Goneril briefly discuss these events. She orders the Fool to go after his master. He does

so, but only after delivering a nasty little piece of doggerel verse on daughters.

322–330: Finally, a proper discussion between Albany and Goneril. Albany provides a voice of moderation, but trusts in his wife's judgement of her father. Note her political reasoning.

331–347: Reference to Oswald and a letter he is to convey from Goneril to Regan. He leaves to take it to Regan's castle. Albany expresses more reservations, which Goneril ignores.

I.v.

1–5: Lear, Kent and the Fool. In prose, Lear orders Kent to take a letter to Regan. Kent leaves.

6–51: Quick, sharp conversation between Lear and the Fool. More signs of Lear losing his wits.

II.i.

1–13: Edmund meets Curan, a minor courtier. They exchange greetings, then Curan tells Edmund about potential conflict between the dukes, as well as the fact that Cornwall will be arriving that night. This is an important little setpiece because it implies an atmosphere of rumours, in which minor courtiers have a better idea of what is going on than perhaps they should. Curan then leaves, presumably on business.

14–19: Switch to poetry, as Edmund makes a little Machiavel-type speech.

20–33: Edmund calls in Edgar and warns him about their father's preparations against him. Edgar believes him, and they 'fight'. Edgar flees.

34–36: Edmund makes some more comments to the audience and then wounds himself, as a visual means of reinforcing his manipulation of Gloucester.

37–85: Gloucester arrives and is completely fooled by Edmund's vocabulary, which uses elements of

Gloucester's own earlier references to signs and unnatural events. Gloucester proscribes Edgar's life.

86–117: Cornwall and Regan arrive with their attendants. Conversation in general about Edgar's 'treachery'. Note Regan's attempt to link Edgar with the riotous behaviour of Lear's men described in an earlier letter from Goneril. Cornwall likes Edmund.

118–129: Cornwall begins to talk about affairs of state to Gloucester, but is cut off by Regan. She describes the problems of contradictory letters. They all leave to go indoors at Gloucester's residence.

II.ii.

1–42: Verbal and then physical violence between Kent and Oswald. Note especially Kent's view of the kind of courtier that has come into existence with the new order of Goneril and Regan (and, soon, Edmund).

44–71: The whole household and the guests all turn up because of the noise. They try to find out what has happened.

72–84: Kent responds in verse; note again his view of the courtier.

85–94: More questions in prose from various people. Kent insults them all.

95–108: Cornwall replies by attacking Kent's kind of courtier. Kent responds by poetic invocation to Apollo and Cornwall doesn't understand him.

108–113: Switch back to prose as Kent responds to Cornwall.

114–132: Switch to poetry as Kent insults them all again and is sentenced by Cornwall to be put in the stocks. Kent points out the grave insult this would be to the King.

133–138: Cornwall doesn't care and Regan increases the penalty. Note reference to Lear's men by Cornwall.

139–147: Gloucester echoes Kent's warning.

147–151:   Cornwall responds by taking full responsibility. Regan then stresses the greater importance of Goneril's messenger. They all leave except Kent and Gloucester.

152–159:   Gloucester expresses his sorrow to Kent and then leaves, with forebodings that the King will not respond kindly to this; Cornwall is wrong.

160–172:   Soliloquy by Kent; note letter from Cordelia. Reference to tragic drama with fortune's wheel at line 160.

II.iii.

1–21:   Important soliloquy by Edgar. Positioning in the narrative is important here: the two honest noblemen are victimised in turn. Edgar states that he is forced to become a kind of Machiavel himself. This would be reinforced by the fact that both would be seen on the Renaissance stage at the same time, with Kent in his stocks.

II.iv.

1–4:   Lear, one of his retainers and the Fool all enter. Lear is discussing with the gentleman his puzzlement at the movements of Regan and Cornwall.

4:   Kent interrupts them.

5–6:   Lear's shock.

7–11:   The Fool's response.

12–27:   Lear refuses to believe that his messenger would be treated in this manner. Note especially his incredulous use of the Royal 'we'.

27–45:   Kent switches to poetry to reinforce his full explanation.

46–55:   Note that it is the Fool who responds first, with a nasty series of comments. This is important, because it shows that Lear is being silenced.

56–60:	Lear finally responds, but in terms of approaching madness. He asks Kent where Regan and Cornwall might be and then goes out to find them.
61–87:	Conversation between Kent and the Fool. More of the Fool's topsy-turvy wisdom, again at Kent's expense.
88–91:	Lear re-enters with Gloucester; he is unable to help. Switch to verse.
91–95:	Lear tries to get access to Regan and Cornwall through Gloucester and fails; his vocabulary becomes incoherent.
96–120:	Lear gives orders to Gloucester and speaks of his control over his subjects. It should by now be apparent that the more he talks of his power, the less he has. Gloucester leaves, trying to keep the peace.
121:	Lear begins to ramble again.
122–126:	The Fool's comments.
127:	Gloucester brings in Cornwall and Regan, as well as some of their attendants. Courtesies are exchanged and Kent is freed.
128–164:	Crucial conversation between Lear and Regan; he continually vilifies Goneril, while she (still mildly, at this point) defends her. Note Cornwall's disbelief at Lear's curses.
165–168:	Lear again curses Goneril horribly.
168–169:	Regan's prophetic comment.
170–181:	Lear reassures her that he will never do the same to her.
181:	Regan, obviously exasperated by all this, wants to know Lear's business. Clear-headed politics again.
182:	Lear asks who put Kent in the stocks but is interrupted by a trumpet announcing a new arrival.
182–187:	Regan recognises Goneril's signal and refers again to a letter. Oswald has entered ahead of Goneril and Lear curses him too. Cornwall is also exasperated.

188–189:   Lear repeats his question and is interrupted again, this time by Goneril's arrival.

189–194:   Lear invokes the heavens and then responds incredulously to Regan's welcome of Goneril.

195–197:   Goneril insults him.

197–198:   Lear starts to go mad again, but finds the patience to ask his question about Kent for the third time.

199–200:   Cornwall admits to it. Lear responds in disbelief.

201:        Regan tries to shut Lear up.

202–263:   Lear going more and more mad, as he has to bargain with his two daughters for his own court.

264–286:   Crucial speech by Lear as he realises his powerlessness and curses both daughters. He leaves in fury, followed by Gloucester, Kent and the Fool. A great storm breaks, in more ways than one.

287–309:   Gloucester returns. The two sisters and Cornwall shut out the King and go off to bed.

III.i.

1–17:   Kent and a Gentleman enter separately. Offstage representation of prior events; Shakespeare changes the method of exposition.

17–42:   Representation of offstage division between Cornwall and Albany.

42–55:   The conversation continues and Kent reveals that he is in contact with Cordelia. They leave separately.

III.ii.

1–36:   Lear's speeches in the midst of the storm as he goes insane. Note prose interruptions of the Fool. Lear acknowledges his complete powerlessness, with a distinct correspondence to Cordelia as Griselda.

| 37–78: | Kent enters and attempts to persuade Lear to take shelter. The King continues his tirade. Note especially the Fool's comments. |
| 79–95: | Kent and Lear leave. The Fool speaks his world-upside-down prophecy. |

III.iii.

| 1–20: | Prose between Gloucester and Edmund. The father refers to Cornwall's treatment of the King as unnatural, and confides to Edmund that he is going to help Lear. He also mentions the division between the dukes. He then leaves. |
| 21–25: | Edmund as Machiavel in poetry. |

III.iv.

1–5:	Kent tries to persuade Lear to take shelter again; note his vocabulary of tyranny. Lear is still preoccupied with his wits.
6–37:	Lear makes explicit comparison between the storm and the tempest in his mind. He then realises that power and ceremony are useless and makes a possibly democratic speech.
38–45:	Interruption in the form of offstage action.
46–108:	Edgar appears, playing the part of a madman. Switch to prose here, although occasionally Lear still uses poetry. Edgar's attack on courtiership is important.
109:	Lear goes completely mad and strips off.
110–113:	The Fool talks sense.
114–124:	Gloucester enters and Edgar pretends to see him as a devil.
125–128:	Kent and Gloucester ask useless questions.
129–148:	Edgar continues his impersonation and eventually Gloucester invites them all into shelter.
149–184:	Multiple simultaneous conversations. Eventually they all go into the hovel.

III.v.

1–25:   Edmund and Cornwall. Edmund's vocabulary of nature again. Note the use of the letter.

III.vi.

1–5:   Prose. Dramatic irony in Kent's farewell to Gloucester.

6–18:   Various bits of nonsense.

19–85:   Insane trial scene. Note Edgar's aside.

86–101:   Gloucester re-enters and gives Kent advice about how to help the King escape to Dover. Everyone leaves except Edgar.

102–115:   Edgar's soliloquy.

III.vii.

1–12:   The real powers in the land come on to the stage. Various preparations for war with the King of France, in prose. Note that this is the first time the audience hears about the invasion. Again, importance of letters.

13–22:   Oswald enters with news of the King's departure. He leaves with Goneril and Edmund.

22–27:   Cornwall's version of justice and legality.

27–41:   Gloucester enters and is bound and abused. Note especially his reference to the codes of hospitality.

42–55:   The second trial scene. Use of letters again.

56–72:   Gloucester replies and Cornwall rips out one of his eyes.

72–82:   Cornwall interrupted by one of his own servants. Cornwall is wounded and Regan kills the servant.

83–98:   Cornwall gouges out Gloucester's other eye and Regan tells him of Edmund's role. Gloucester is led off and Regan exits with her bleeding husband.

99–107:   Choral function of the servants.

IV.i.

1–9: Edgar's soliloquy, again on flattering courtiership.

9–50: Gloucester enters, led by an old man. Note Edgar's asides. The old man leaves Gloucester in the care of 'Poor Tom'.

51–79: Gloucester asks Edgar to take him to the top of the Dover cliffs.

IV.ii.

1–19: Goneril and Edmund enter and Goneril comments on the fact that her husband has not come out to meet them. Oswald then enters with news of Albany's state of mind. Oswald seems incredulous that Albany is not happy with the new world order. Note the careful offstage preparation technique again here.

19–25: Goneril declares her love for Edmund; he then leaves.

26–28: Goneril compares Edmund and Albany.

29–69: Albany enters. Verbal violence: Goneril vs. Albany. She attacks him, vilifying his manhood in comparison to how she thinks a man should act.

69–97: News arrives of Gloucester's blinding and Cornwall's death offstage. Letters again. Note Goneril's aside.

IV.iii.

1–55: Kent and the Gentleman enter in mid-conversation. Another opportunity for offstage representation. The audience finds out that the King of France has had to return home because of his own problems. Cordelia is explicitly referred to as a Griselda figure in preparation for her return to the stage.

IV.iv.

1–29:	Cordelia in the French camp. Discussion between her and a doctor, as well as signs of war.

IV.v.

1–40:	Regan and Oswald discuss the war: more offstage representation. Regan tries to suborn her sister's servant in the matter of the struggle over Edmund.

IV.vi.

1–10:	Gloucester is misled by Edgar so that his intended suicide bid should not succeed. Prose here.
11–41:	Switch to verse, which Gloucester realises in his reference to Edgar's different accents. Gloucester prays to the gods and then attempts suicide. Note Edgar's aside at lines 33–34.
41–80:	The aftermath; Edgar in a new guise persuades his father that he has been delivered by the heavens.
80–107:	Lear enters dressed as the King of Misrule; note that he speaks in prose.
107–129:	Lear switches to verse in response to Gloucester's recognition. Crucial speech on the nature of kingship.
130–187:	Important conversation between the two old men.
188–203:	The French arrive and attempt to catch Lear, who runs off as though he were being hunted: reversal of the Wild Hunt?
204–226:	News of impending battle.
226–250:	Fight between Edgar and Oswald; Oswald is killed.
251–270:	Edgar reads a letter carried by Oswald.
271–286:	Edgar's response. He then takes his father to safety as the muster for battle is heard offstage.

IV.vii.

1–11:	Cordelia thanks Kent for his loyal service.
12–23:	The doctor and Cordelia discuss her father's case.
24–84:	Reconciliation.
85–96:	Report of impending battle.

V.i.

1–17:	Conversation between Regan and Edmund; note that he swears by his honour at line 14.
17–36:	Goneril and Albany arrive with their contingent. Discussion about the battle plan. Note Goneril's asides about Regan.
37–50:	As they all leave Edgar, in disguise, calls to Albany. He presents him with the letter he took from Oswald and asks him to sound a challenge on its contents after the battle. He refuses to identify himself and then exits.
51–54:	Edmund enters with news that the battle is about to begin. Albany leaves.
55–69:	Edmund's soliloquy.

V.ii.

1–11:	Short scene between Edgar and his father as the battle rages offstage.

V.iii.

1–25:	Aftermath of the battle. Lear and Cordelia comfort each other after the defeat and are led away to prison.
26–39:	Edmund's orders to the Captain to murder Lear and Cordelia. Note use of a letter again. The Captain leaves to do the deed.
40–61:	The rest of the army enters, along with the two sisters and Albany. He commends Edmund on his performance and asks what he has done with the captives. Edmund replies that he has sent them to prison. Albany notes the difference in rank between Edmund and himself.

61–66: Regan uses the Royal 'we' and prefers Edmund, perhaps with a further allusion to her intention of marrying him in her description of him as being, in effect, Albany's brother.

67–72: Nasty little spat between the two sisters over Edmund.

73–82: Regan announces that she intends to marry Edgar, but she also mentions that she is not feeling well. More nastiness between the two sisters. Albany insults Edmund's breeding, but Regan challenges this.

82–106: Albany accuses Edmund of treason; Goneril responds to it as part of a play. Albany challenges Edmund, if no other comes forth. Regan falls ill and, in an aside to the audience, Goneril admits that she has poisoned her sister. Regan is led off ill.

107–151: The challenge is proclaimed and Edgar enters in disguise to answer it. He refuses to reveal his true name, but Edmund chooses to fight him anyway. Edmund is fatally wounded.

152–161: Albany tries to silence Goneril by showing her the letter. She brazens it out by direct reference to pure power polities. Albany challenges her again and she leaves in distraction.

162–181: Edmund admits to everything and Edgar reveals himself.

182–200: Edgar relates the offstage death of his father.

200–222: Edmund is about to do some good, perhaps by telling what he has ordered the Captain to do, but he lets Edgar continue: obvious audience manipulation by tension here. Edgar relates how he met Kent and the truth about the latter's service to the King.

222–230: News of the deaths of the two sisters offstage.

230–242: Kent enters and, after various greetings, Edmund gives the reasons for the deaths of the two sisters.

243–257:   Edmund tells the nobles what he has ordered to be done to the prisoners; Edgar leaves, but too late to save them. Edmund is carried off.

258–280:   Lear enters bearing Cordelia dead in his arms; the others all follow him. The only thing Lear now cares about is the fact that she is dead. He even tried to save her by killing the Captain who hanged her.

281–295:   Kent is revealed to Lear.

296–312:   Edmund's offstage death is reported and Lear relates that his Fool has been hanged. He fancies that Cordelia is alive, and then dies.

313–327:   Typical aftermath of tragedy, with the survivors forced to bear witness.

Discussion Points

1. Narrative patternings: the relationships between the Gloucester subplot and the main plot.
2. Two world views: the old court of Lear, Gloucester and Kent versus the new court of Goneril, Regan, Cornwall, Edmund and Oswald. Feudal versus Renaissance?
3. The use of letters.
4. The language of nature. It seems to change its meanings, depending on who uses it.
5. The family.
6. Women, speech and power.
7. The mythological significance of the play: paganism.
8. The world upside down: the Fool and the topsy-turvy King of Misrule.
9. Lear's vocabulary of monsters.
10. Madness, foolishness and playing the madman: Lear, the Fool and Edgar.
11. The scenic structure and varying the method of exposition.

15

Course Materials: *Hamlet*

Hamlet is perhaps the most studied of Shakespeare's plays. This chapter will provide a breakdown of the play that should prove very helpful to students at any level. The play in its modern edited form is very long and complex, so a breakdown of the action is a useful thing to have. It should help structure your study and enable you to make sense of any lectures you are given on the play, as well as helping you to formulate issues for tutorial discussion.

The chapter has:

■ A breakdown of the entire play, divided by act and scene
■ Discussion points

Play Breakdown

I.i.

1–13:	Two sentries (Barnardo and Francisco) enter and exchange greetings.
14–17:	Horatio and Marcellus enter; they should appear to be of superior rank to the sentries. Francisco leaves.
17–39:	The three discuss something terrible that has been seen on previous nights.
40–51:	The Ghost enters, looking like the dead king. It leaves when Horatio orders it to speak.
52–125:	Horatio, Marcellus and Barnardo discuss what they have just seen. This is important because of the way it sets out the action prior to the play for the audience.
126–141:	The ghost comes on again and leaves as dawn breaks.

142–175:   More discussion. Horatio and Marcellus decide to tell young Prince Hamlet what they have seen. All leave.

I.ii.

1–41:   The whole Danish court arrives in state. Claudius enacts business, sending two courtiers, Voltemand and Cornelius, as messengers to Fortinbras of Norway.

42–63:   Claudius deals next with Laertes and Polonius.

64–128:   Interaction between Hamlet, Claudius and Gertrude. Hamlet's isolation is marked by the use of the aside. The court leaves, Hamlet staying behind on his own.

129–159:   Hamlet's first soliloquy, intimating to the audience that something is wrong – perhaps with himself, or perhaps with the transfer of power and his mother's marriage to Claudius after old Hamlet's sudden death.

160–253:   Horatio, Marcellus and Barnardo enter and relate what they have seen. Hamlet questions them in detail and arranges to watch with them. They leave him on his own.

254–257:   Hamlet's little epilogue to the scene.

I.iii.

1–51:   Conversation between Laertes and Ophelia.

52–87:   Polonius enters and gives Laertes his blessing. Laertes leaves to return to his studies in France.

87–136:   Polonius turns to Ophelia and tries to find out what, if anything, has passed between her and Hamlet. He orders her to become colder to the young prince. She acquiesces and they both leave.

I.iv.

1–38:   Night. Hamlet, Horatio and Marcellus enter.

38–57:   The Ghost enters and beckons to Hamlet to follow it.

58–86:   Horatio and Marcellus try to persuade Hamlet not to go. He defies them and leaves with the Ghost.

87–91:   The other two follow after.

I.v.

1–91:   The Ghost reveals all to Hamlet, urging him to vengeance.

92–114:   The Ghost leaves and Hamlet delivers his second long soliloquy.

114–149:   Horatio and Marcellus catch up with Hamlet – already his language shows signs of the 'antic disposition'.

149–190:   Hamlet makes the other two swear never to tell anyone else about what they have seen, aided by exhortations from the Ghost from offstage. Hamlet leaves together with the two others.

II.i.

1–70:   Polonius gives orders to Reynaldo; Polonius is tending towards the tedious by this point. Reynaldo leaves.

71–117:   Ophelia comes in and relates her strange encounter with Hamlet to her father. Polonius decides to tell Claudius and leaves with his daughter.

II.ii.

1–39:   Claudius enters with Gertrude and two of Hamlet's student friends, Rosencrantz and Guildenstern. He relates how Hamlet's behaviour worries him and sets them to watch over him. They leave in order to do so.

41–57:   Polonius enters, announcing the return of the two ambassadors to Fortinbras. He also tells the King and Queen that he thinks he has found the reason for Hamlet's behaviour. Representation

	of offstage events here. Polonius exits to usher in Voltemand and Cornelius.
58–84:	State business dealt with, the ambassadors leave.
85–170:	Polonius, Claudius and Gertrude discuss Hamlet. Note Gertrude's impatience with Polonius. They see Hamlet in the distance and decide that Gertrude and Claudius should hide behind an arras to see how he interacts with Polonius. The two of them leave as Hamlet comes on.
170–221:	Hamlet fools with Polonius, who leaves just as Rosencrantz and Guildenstern come on.
222–379:	Prose conversation between Hamlet and the two students. Note the various asides as they all watch one another's responses.
380–420:	Polonius comes back on and announces the arrival of the actors. Hamlet makes fun of him.
421–549:	Some of the actors arrive; complicated interaction. The players agree to put on a play with material inserted by Hamlet. Everyone leaves except Hamlet.
549–605:	Hamlet's third soliloquy, explaining to the audience how he intends to use the play to see Claudius' reaction. He exits.

III.i.

1–28:	Claudius, Gertrude, Ophelia and Polonius enter with Rosencrantz and Guildenstern. Claudius and Gertrude question the two students and then Claudius sends them off to continue spying on Hamlet.
28–41:	Claudius asks Gertrude to leave while he and Polonius hide. The plan is to see what happens when Hamlet meets Ophelia. Gertrude exits.
42–54:	Claudius and Polonius set up the scene. Note Claudius' aside on his conscience. They leave Ophelia alone; the convention here is that the two men will see what is happening from offstage.

55–87:	Hamlet enters, with his 'To be or not to be' soliloquy. Note that this is technically not a soliloquy, since Ophelia is also onstage.
87–149:	Switch to prose as Hamlet encounters Ophelia. After some more of his weird behaviour, he exits.
150–161:	Ophelia's soliloquy on Hamlet's behaviour. She withdraws to a different part of the stage as Claudius and Polonius come back.
162–178:	Conversation between Claudius and Polonius. The King is certain that there is more going on with Hamlet than just love madness, and begins to work out ways to ensure that it will not endanger his state. Presumably Ophelia is not supposed to overhear this discussion – technique of simultaneous staging.
178–188:	Ophelia joins the two men and they all leave.

III.ii.

1–45:	Hamlet enters with three of the players. Prose conversation. The actors leave.
46–50:	Polonius enters with Rosencrantz and Guildenstern. Hamlet makes sure that Claudius will be present at the play. The three others leave him alone onstage.
51–89:	Hamlet calls for Horatio, who enters. Hamlet asks him to keep an eye on Claudius during the play.
90–140:	The court enters and settles for the play. The plot is foretold by means of a dumb show.
141–154:	The Prologue enters and speaks, while Hamlet makes comments to Ophelia.
155–270:	The mousetrap play within a play. Note the running commentary by Hamlet. Claudius starts up when he sees the play's action and the whole court leaves in confusion, with Hamlet and Horatio staying behind.
271–295:	Hamlet and Horatio discuss what has just happened.

296–344:	Switch to prose. Rosencrantz and Guildenstern enter and tell Hamlet that his mother wishes to speak with him in private. Hamlet makes fun of them.
345–372:	The players enter and play music – Hamlet uses this to comment upon the efforts of Rosencrantz and Guildenstern.
373–387:	Polonius enters to repeat the message that Gertrude wants to speak with Hamlet and gets short shrift from the Prince. Hamlet tells everyone to leave him alone.
388–399:	Revenger's soliloquy by Hamlet.

III.iii.

1–26:	Claudius enters in discussion with Rosencrantz and Guildenstern. They leave him as Polonius enters.
27–35:	Polonius tells Claudius that Hamlet is going to see Gertrude and that he will conceal himself in order to see what happens. He leaves to do so.
36–72:	Claudius' soliloquy admitting his guilt. He kneels to pray.
72–96:	Hamlet arrives and sees the King alone and in prayer. He has the opportunity to enact his revenge, but decides not to do so because he wants total revenge on Claudius's soul as well as his body. Hamlet leaves to go to his mother's apartments.
97–98:	Concluding couplet by Claudius, who then exits.

III.iv.

1–7:	Gertrude and Polonius. He tells her that he will hide and watch what happens.
8–24:	The closet scene. Hamlet enters and makes Gertrude sit with him. The use of force frightens her and she cries out for help. Polonius starts at the noise; Hamlet notices this and thrusts his sword through the arras, killing Polonius.

25–33:	Hamlet hopes that it is Claudius whom he has killed, but draws the arras to see Polonius' body instead.
34–101:	Hamlet's words to his mother.
101–136:	The Ghost enters to remind Hamlet of his purpose and tells him not to take it out on Gertrude. She does not see the apparition, but she does see Hamlet talking to it and thinks he's mad. The Ghost exits.
137–217:	Long conversation between Hamlet and Gertrude, mostly by the son. They leave separately, Hamlet dragging off Polonius' body.

IV.ii.

1–4:	Hamlet enters, having hidden Polonius' body.
5–31:	Rosencrantz and Guildenstern come on and try to find out where Hamlet has hidden the body. He makes sarcastic fun of their attempts. All three leave.

IV.iii.

1–11:	Claudius with some servants. He comments on the effects of Hamlet's condition.
11–15:	Rosencrantz enters and tells Claudius that Hamlet is under guard, although he will not tell where he has put the body.
16–39:	Through his 'madness' Hamlet finally tells where he has hidden it; the attendants leave to find it.
40–57:	Claudius tells Hamlet that he is to leave for England. Hamlet exits, quickly followed by Rosencrantz and Guildenstern.
58–68:	Claudius in soliloquy lets the audience know what his plan is – to have Hamlet executed when he lands in England.

IV.iv.

1–8:	The Norwegian army passes over the stage. A single captain stays behind.

9–29:   Enter Hamlet, Rosencrantz and Guildenstern. Conversation with the captain, who leaves.

30–31:   Hamlet sends the others ahead.

32–66:   Hamlet's revenge soliloquy.

IV.v.

1–20:   Gertrude, Horatio and one of the courtiers discuss the state of Ophelia. Offstage representation here.

21–36:   Ophelia's first mad scene.

37–74:   Everyone tries to humour her. Eventually she leaves and Claudius orders Horatio to go and keep an eye on her.

75–96:   Claudius bemoans what has happened to Ophelia.

96–116:   Confusion reigns as Laertes bursts in with the support of the commoners. He persuades them to stay outside while he talks with the King.

115–154:   Three-way discussion between Laertes, Claudius and Gertrude.

155–201:   Ophelia interrupts them; second part of her madness performance. Eventually she leaves.

202–220:   Laertes agrees to have a private audience with Claudius.

IV.vi.

1–6:   Horatio comes in with a gentleman who says some sailors have letters for him.

7–33:   Horatio reads a letter from Hamlet.

IV.vii.

1–35:   Claudius begins to negotiate with Laertes.

36–162:   They are interrupted by the arrival of a letter from Hamlet for Claudius. They then conspire together against Hamlet.

163–193:   They are interrupted again, this time by the noise of the people offstage. Gertrude arrives to tell them that Ophelia is dead. All leave.

V.i.

1–217:   The 'gravedigger' scene.

218–265:   Ophelia's funeral. Both Hamlet and Laertes end up in her grave, fighting.

266–293:   Everyone tries to calm them down. Hamlet leaves, followed by Horatio at the King's command.

294–299:   Claudius and Laertes seal their deal and all leave.

V.ii.

1–80:   Hamlet tells Horatio everything that happened to him while abroad.

81–181:   Osric the courtier arrives and Hamlet makes a whole series of vicious comments about him. Osric as emblem of the court? Osric finally leaves after Hamlet agrees to a mock duel with Laertes.

181–194:   Some more comments by Hamlet.

195–224:   One of the lords enters to repeat the invitation and leaves to give Hamlet's assent to Claudius. Hamlet philosophises.

225–280:   The court enters and Hamlet scores the first hit in the duel.

281–292:   Hamlet scores another hit. In the meantime, Gertrude drinks from a goblet poisoned by Claudius as extra insurance.

293–302:   The duel continues. Laertes finally scores a hit on Hamlet with the poisoned rapier. Angered by being struck by a pointed weapon, Hamlet presses Laertes, who drops his rapier. Hamlet then wounds Laertes with his own sharpened (and poisoned) weapon.

302–322:   Confusion as Gertrude dies and Laertes tells Hamlet about the poisoned rapier. Hamlet uses it to strike Claudius as well.

322–331:   Both Claudius and Laertes die.

| 332–360: | Hamlet dies after asking Horatio to tell all; in the meantime the Norwegians arrive. |
| 361–402: | Finale with Fortinbras. |

Discussion Points

1. Emblematic staging.
2. Social rank.
3. Stage techniques – asides, soliloquies, simultaneous staging.
4. Representation of offstage events and persons.
5. Structure. Shorts scenes vs. long scenes.
6. Horatio as chorus figure.

16 Course Materials: *Macbeth*

One-minute overview

This chapter deals with the last of the Shakespeare plays you are most likely to encounter before getting to Honours-level study. *Macbeth* is also the play you are most likely to come across if you are going through the Scottish education system, from secondary school onward.

In this chapter you will find:

■ A breakdown of the entire play, divided by act and scene
■ Discussion points

Play Breakdown

I.i.

1–12:   The witches enact a short prologue scene.

I.ii.

1–44:   Report of battle relayed to King Duncan. Note that his warfare is always enacted by and through others. Banquo and Macbeth are both reported to be great warriors and leaders.

45–67:   News of a second battle reported to the King. He orders Rosse and Angus to tell Macbeth of his reward, the title of 'Thane of Cawdor'. Note that Macbeth is offstage throughout; he is made known to the audience by means of others' descriptions of him.

I.iii.

1–37:   The second witches' scene.

38–78:   Macbeth and Banquo enter and encounter the witches. They speak their prophecy about the two men's greatness and then vanish.

79–88:   Macbeth and Banquo discuss what they have just seen.

89–156: Rosse and Angus enter with the news of Macbeth's new title. He and Banquo discuss it in relation to the witches' prophecy in a series of asides. All leave for court.

I.iv.

1–14:   Duncan's court. The death of the former Thane of Cawdor is reported.

14–58:   Macbeth, Banquo, Rosse and Angus arrive, just in time to see Malcolm being invested with the title of Prince of Cumberland – heir to the throne. Note Macbeth's comment aside on this as he leaves.

I.v.

1–29:   Lady Macbeth reads a letter from her husband relating the witches' prophecy and subsequent events. Note her comment on her husband's character.

29–38:   A messenger arrives to tell her of the imminent arrival of Macbeth and Duncan. She orders the messenger to greet Macbeth.

38–54:   Lady Macbeth's invocation speech.

54–72:   Macbeth enters and is greeted by his wife. Brief discussion; she tells him to leave everything up to her as she begins the plot.

I.vi.

1–10:   Duncan arrives with the court.

10–31:   Lady Macbeth welcomes them all and conducts them into the castle.

I.vii.

1–28:   Preparations. Macbeth enters and speaks his soliloquy on ambition.

28–82:   Crucial interaction as Lady Macbeth enters to encourage her husband.

II.i.

1–9:   Banquo and his son Fleance in the dark.

10–32:   Macbeth enters a servant and asks Banquo to meet him later to discuss the witches' prophecy. He agrees and leaves with Fleance. Macbeth orders his servant to go to Lady Macbeth and then go to bed. The servant exits, leaving Macbeth alone onstage for the second time.

33–64:   Macbeth's soliloquy as he prepares to go and kill Duncan.

II.ii.

1–54:   Confused interaction between the Macbeths. He has killed Duncan, but still has the daggers. His wife leaves to frame Duncan's attendants. Note the insistent vocabulary of conscience that impinges every so often.

54–71:   Knocking at the castle's main door disturbs Macbeth's state of mind even more. His wife enters to take him to their chamber in order to wash off the blood and appear innocent. They leave to do so.

II.iii.

1–42:   The 'porter' scene: gallows humour as Macduff and Lennox arrive at the castle.

42–52:   Macbeth arrives, ostensibly awakened by the arrival of the two nobles.

52–63:   Macduff leaves to wake the King. Lennox relates the terrible night that has just passed.

63–118:	Confusion as Macduff comes back with news of the King's murder. People arrive in groups to find out what is going on; Lady Macbeth faints.
119–125:	Duncan's sons Malcolm and Donalbain discuss in asides what to do while everyone else is distracted; they decide to flee later.
125–134:	Banquo suggests an investigation into the event and everyone leaves except Donalbain and Malcolm.
135–146:	They openly discuss their options. Donalbain decides to flee to Ireland; Malcolm notes that more murder could be intended (they are, after all, Duncan's sons) and both of them leave the castle as fast as possible.

II.iv.

| 1–19: | Rosse and an old man enter, discussing more signs and portents. |
| 19–41: | Macduff enters with news that Macbeth has killed Duncan's two servants, who seemed to have done the deed. Also, the King's sons have fled, casting suspicion on themselves in the process. |

III.i.

1–10:	Banquo's soliloquy as he refers to the prophecy – and his suspicions about Macbeth.
11–39:	Macbeth's court enters. He invites Banquo to a feast that evening. Banquo replies that he is taking Fleance riding during the afternoon, but will be back in time for the feast. Banquo exits.
40–43:	Macbeth bids everyone else to leave and entertain themselves as they wish until the feast. They all leave apart from Macbeth and one servant.
44–47:	Macbeth sends the servant to bring in the men who are waiting outside the gates.
46–71:	Macbeth's soliloquy on the threat posed by Banquo.

72–141: The servant returns with two desperate men; Macbeth orders his servant out while he talks with them about murdering Banquo.

III.ii.

1–4: Lady Macbeth sends a servant to Macbeth.
4–7: Epigrammatic utterance by Lady Macbeth.
8–56: Macbeth enters; conversation between the two of them. He is beginning to pull away from her influence, planning deeds without telling her.

III.iii.

1–14: Three murderers enter – the third has been added by Macbeth to watch over the other two.
14–18: Banquo and Fleance enter; confusion as Banquo is killed. Fleance escapes.
19–21: The murderers leave to report back to Macbeth.

III.iv.

1–8: The court enters for the banquet.
9–31: Macbeth deals with one of the murderers at a side door. He is told that Banquo is dead but Fleance has escaped. He is not at all happy about this, and tells the man that they will discuss the matter further the next day.
31–36: Lady Macbeth ushers her husband back to the table.
36–72: Banquo's ghost sits in Macbeth's place; he sees it and confuses everyone by talking about something no one else can see. Note Lady Macbeth's gendered language as she rebukes her husband. The ghost leaves.
72–87: They try to get the banquet back on track.
88–106: The ghost re-enters; more confusion as the feast is disrupted even more. The ghost leaves.
106–120: The feast breaks up and everyone leaves except Macbeth and his wife.

121–143: Conversation between the Macbeths. Hints of more mayhem to come as he begins to plot against Macduff and thinks of going to see the witches again.

III.v.

1–36: The witches and Hecate discuss Macbeth. This scene was probably inserted by a different dramatist and is usually cut in performance.

III.vi.

1–49: Representation of offstage events in Macbeth's kingdom by Lennox in conversation with another lord. The most important piece of information is that war is brewing with England; Malcolm and Macduff are both there.

IV.i.

1–38: The witches and their cauldron.

39–44: Hecate comes in with more of the coven. They sing a charm around the cauldron and then Hecate leaves.

45–68: Macbeth enters and demands more knowledge from the witches.

69–103: The three apparitions and prophecy. Macbeth orders the witches to show him more.

104–132: They show him the line of Stuart kings descended from Banquo and Fleance and then all vanish, leaving Macbeth alone.

133–134: His curse on them.

135–156: Lennox interrupts. Note Macbeth's murderous aside.

IV.ii.

1–29: Scene at Macduff's castle. Rosse tries to comfort Macduff's wife and son, but the times are dangerous and he leaves.

30–63:	Cute domestic chatter between mother and son.
64–73:	A messenger arrives and warns them. He leaves quickly, for the same reasons as Rosse.
73–79:	Lady Macduff's helplessness.
79–85:	Macbeth's henchmen arrive and the massacre begins.

IV.iii.

1–139:	Scene in England between Malcolm and Macduff. Malcolm deliberately tests Macduff's patience.
140–159:	Description of Edward the Confessor and his saintliness. Note that in reality he was one of the weakest kings England has ever had, as well as being an utterly inept politician.
159–240:	Rosse arrives with word of the massacre of Macduff's family. He has trouble speaking of what happened. Macduff bewails what has happened and then swears revenge. Notice the gendered language here.

V.i.

1–79:	Lady Macbeth's sleepwalking scene as she is watched over by one of her gentlewoman and a doctor.

V.ii.

1–31:	Many of the Scottish nobles defect to Malcolm with their forces.

V.iii.

1–10:	Macbeth's defiance as he enters with some servants and the doctor.
11–29:	A messenger arrives with news of the English army. Macbeth berates him and sends him out. He then calls for Seyton.
30–60:	Seyton helps arm Macbeth, who keeps muttering about Dunsinane. Meanwhile the doctor reports

on Lady Macbeth's mental state. Everyone leaves except the doctor.

61–62: The doctor deserts as well.

V.iv.

1–21: The Scots rebels meet up with the invasion force.

V.v.

1–8: Macbeth and Seyton enter with troops. A cry is heard from the castle's women offstage. Seyton goes to see what is happening.

9–15: Macbeth's reckless lack of fear.

15–28: Seyton reports Lady Macbeth's offstage death. Macbeth utters his speech on mortality with theatrical metaphors.

28–51: A messenger enters with the strange news of a moving wood. Macbeth berates him, but the messenger stands firm. They leave for battle.

V.vi.

1–10: The attackers get ready for the fight.

V.vii.

1–13: Macbeth kills young Siward then exits.

14–23: Macduff comes in, seeking Macbeth, then leaves.

24–29: Malcolm and Siward take possession of Macbeth's stronghold.

V.viii.

1–34: Macbeth and Macduff fight. Macduff tells of his history and Macbeth realises that this is the man who can kill him. Even so he fights to the end as they go offstage, battling.

V.ix.

1–19:	The attacking army enters. Siward is told of his son's death, but is pleased that he died fighting bravely.
20–24:	Macduff comes in with Macbeth's head.
24–41:	Finale as Malcolm is proclaimed King.

Discussion Points

1. The witches.
2. Destiny and free will.
3. The presentation of the two courts: Duncan's Scotland vs. Macbeth's.
4. Gender.
5. Representation of offstage events and persons.
6. Structure: the scene sequences, from short to long.
7. Versions of history.

Index